WANDA & BRUNSTETTER'S
Amish Friends
OUTDOOR
COOKBOOK

BARBOUR
PUBLISHING

Published by Barbour Publishing, Inc., 1810 Barbour Drive, Uhrichsville, Ohio 44683, www.barbourbooks.com

Our mission is to inspire the world with the life-changing message of the Bible.

Printed in China.

INTRODUCTION

During my growing-up years, my parents often took my sister and me on camping trips to the mountains or to the beach in Washington. The four of us enjoyed meals prepared either over a fire or on a portable gas stove. At home my father, an experienced hunter and fisherman, liked to cook a variety of meats on his outdoor grill. Fresh salmon that he'd caught in the Pacific Ocean was one of his favorite things to grill. I have fond memories of those special days.

Most of my Amish friends are outdoor enthusiasts. They appreciate nature and enjoy a variety of outdoor activities that often include camping and cooking. Some also like to hunt and fish. On some occasions when my husband and I have eaten at Amish friends' homes, all or part of the meal was cooked on the grill or in a big pot over a slow-burning open fire. I remember one time when we enjoyed some freshly caught fish barbecued on the grill. Another evening we had hot dogs and beans that were cooked over an open fire. Those meals were both delicious.

On several other occasions while visiting Amish friends, we all sat around an open fire and enjoyed some tasty snacks that had been prepared. There was a time of fellowship with visiting, singing, and playing musical instruments. My husband had his guitar, and one of our Amish friends played a harmonica. It's always uplifting to sing songs of praise, especially when we can benefit from being together in the great outdoors.

I hope you will appreciate the variety of more than two hundred tasty recipes in this cookbook that Amish friends have cooked and served outdoors. Also included is advice for prep work, packing a cooler, grilling in foil packs, maintaining cast-iron tools, and much more.

I wish to thank my editor, Rebecca Germany, for seeing that the recipes submitted by Amish friends were compiled in this special outdoor cooking cookbook.

Wanda E. Brunstetter

He makes me to
lie down in green pastures;
He leads me beside the still
waters. He restores my soul.

Psalm 23:2–3

CONTENTS

Editor's Note

O utdoor cooking was once part of everyday life for our ancestors, but today it has become more of a novelty or hobby. Cooking outdoors, though, can remind us of those who paved the way for us and help us connect with the beauty of God's creation.

To get started, you really don't need to buy any fancy equipment. You don't need to travel to a camping location. Your first attempt at outdoor cooking may be roasting hot dogs on a stick in a fire ring in your backyard.

We have organized the recipes contributed here by our Amish friends according to the main tools recommended for use with their recipes. Often you can substitute a grill grate positioned over a campfire built with wood in place of a charcoal or propane gas grill. Similarly, a foil packet of food can be placed in campfire coals instead of on a grill. Skewers for hot dog and marshmallow roasting can be made from straight sticks by whittling one end to a point.

Be creative, but always keep safety in mind. Build your fire away from dry leaves and grasses. Don't build a fire under low-hanging branches or near a structure. Use stones, cement blocks, a truck tire rim, or a purchased fire ring to contain your fire. Don't set a grill too close to a house, camper, or other structure. And always use common sense.

Finally, go with the flow and have fun. After all, what you are really outdoors to make are memories.

O LORD, our Lord,
how excellent is Your name in all the earth,
who have set Your glory above the heavens! . . .
When I consider Your heavens,
the work of Your fingers,
the moon and the stars, which You have ordained,
what is man that You are mindful of him,
and the son of man that You visit him?

PSALM 8:1, 3–4

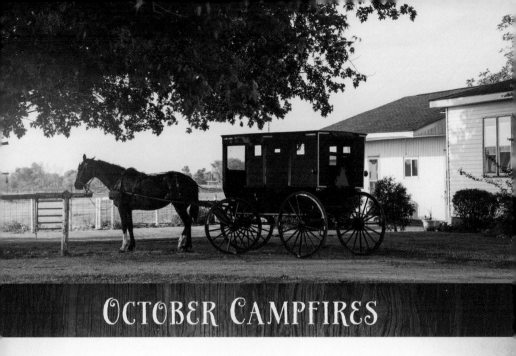

OCTOBER CAMPFIRES

When the leaves turn fiery orange and red and the nights grow cool, we know it's time for our yearly October campfire.

The tradition began some years back with a simple bonfire in a homemade concrete-block firepit as a late Saturday evening supper with an abundance of home-grown burgers, hot dogs, and grillers.

The cheery flames of our fire beckoned first my sister, along with her husband and their three small daughters. Next came my cousins who live almost next door. And finally came my mother who does live next door. They invited themselves to our fire, and our simple meal grew with each new arrival bringing hot chocolate, ingredients for s'mores, chocolate candies, hot meadow tea, and popcorn.

The night air grew cool. We dressed in sweaters and caps and wrapped ourselves in blankets while sipping hot drinks.

The children, tired out from their boisterous hide-and-seek game, gravitated to the bonfire. They cuddled into blankets taken from beds, couches, and carriages and found laps or chairs to sit on. One by one the littlest ones dropped off to sleep.

Finally, the fire low and midnight approaching, we gathered blankets, chairs, dishes, and children. As we parted ways, we knew with certainty a new tradition had been born.

RACHEL STOLTZFUS, **Paradise, PA**

Cooking on a Stick

Many blessings are overlooked because they don't cost us anything.

ANNA A. SLABAUGH, APPLE CREEK, OH

C ooking on a stick is pretty basic, and it is a fun way to involve older children in cooking their food. Simply cut a straight, sturdy tree branch about three feet long. Use a sharp knife to remove the bark on one end and whittle it to a point. Now you have a tool on which to hold your hot dog or marshmallow over a fire. Alternately, purchased stainless steel roasting forks may be used.

When cooking on a stick, you'll want to build a teepee-style fire. In your cleared area, place a pile of tinder (wood shavings, dry leaves, crumpled newspaper, etc.) in the center. Lean small sticks of dry kindling in a circle that meets at the top around the tinder. Light the fire, and when it gets going, add larger sticks then logs to the teepee. This type of fire burns hot and quick, but wait until some coals develop before cooking over it. Holding your food in the flames will char the exterior before the interior is cooked through.

Bucket Fire

If you don't have a firepit, try building a small fire in a galvanized or steel pail set on an 8- to 10-inch-thick chunk of wood. We love to sit in the backyard, roasting hot dogs and eating snacks.

Anna A. Slabaugh, Apple Creek, OH

COOKING on a STICK

Wonderful Wieners

Wieners (hot dogs)
Bacon

Skewer wiener on stick. Wrap bacon strip around wiener. Use toothpicks to secure bacon. Roast over fire until bacon is browned. Eat plain or on bun.

Lizzie Ann Swartzentruber, Newcomerstown, OH
Mrs. Chester (Rose) Miller, Centerville, PA

Bacon-Cheese Dogs

String cheese   Bacon slices
Hot dogs

Carefully slice string cheese lengthwise into four pieces. Cut slit into each hot dog lengthwise. Insert cheese slice into slit of each hot dog. Wrap each hot dog with bacon slice. Secure bacon with toothpicks. Place horizontally on roasting stick. Hold over fire until bacon is cooked through, rotating stick occasionally. Watch for popping bacon grease. Remove from stick and serve with or without bun.

Rhoda Byler, Brookville, PA

Big Dogs

Nothing says campfire food like hot dogs! When you can make a dog and bun in one, it's big dog heaven!

**Hot dogs
Refrigerated breadstick dough**

Wrap strips of breadstick dough around hot dogs mummy-style. Skewer onto sticks and roast slowly over hot coals until nicely browned. Keep rotating for even cooking. Eat hot dogs plain or dip them in ketchup and mustard.

TENA BYLER, Wilcox, PA

Pigs in a Blanket

**Hot dogs
Crescent roll dough**

Thread hot dog onto stick and wrap wedge of crescent dough around hot dog, pressing edges closed. Use toothpicks to secure if needed. Hold over fire until dough is golden brown.

.MRS. GIDEON L. MILLER, Loudonville, OH

Piggies in a Blanket

**Crescent roll dough   Cheese curds
Little smokies**

Spread triangle of crescent dough on plate. Place sausage and cheese curd in center of dough. Roll and seal tightly so cheese doesn't escape. Skewer onto roasting stick and brown slowly over hot coals, turning so dough cooks completely. You'll be a pro in no time. Delicious!

FANNIE STOLTZFUS, Christiana, PA

We use sliced cheese.
KAREN MAST, LaGrange, IN

I do this using my own pizza dough.
MRS. CHESTER (ROSE) MILLER, Centerville, PA

Bologna Rolls

Bologna slices
Cheese slices

Roll cheese slice inside bologna slice. Skewer onto stick. Roast over campfire coals. The bologna will get a little crunchy outside while the cheese melts inside.

BECKY FISHER, Lancaster, PA

Meat on a Stick

You can cook more than just a hot dog on a stick. Try sausage links, smoked sausage chunks, and chicken tenders. You can also make a kebab by alternating chunks of meat between onion, zucchini, cherry tomatoes, mushrooms, peppers, pineapple chunks, and the like.

Bacon on a Stick

Thread strip of bacon onto stick, poking through bacon lengthwise every inch or so. Hold over hot coals until done to desired crispness.

Toasted Cheese

Cut your favorite cheese(s) into 1-inch chunks. Put on hot dog stick and roast over open fire until cheese starts to melt. If desired, sprinkle with salt. Eat with waffle pretzels and/or crackers.

BETTY SUE MILLER, Millersburg, OH

Cut string cheese into thirds and put on roasting sticks. Roast until slightly melted.
JOLENE BONTRAGER, Goshen, IN

Roasted Smokie Jalapeño Poppers

6 jalapeño peppers	12 little smokies
4 ounces cream cheese, softened	12 slices bacon

Place toothpicks in bowl to soak. Set aside. Cut stems off peppers and remove all seeds. If you leave any seeds inside, they will be very hot and spicy. Put 1 to 2 tablespoons of cream cheese inside each pepper along with a little smokie. Press in firmly. Wrap bacon slice around pepper and stick water-soaked toothpick through bacon into pepper to hold in place. Put pepper on roasting fork or stick, and roast over hot coals until bacon is crisp and pepper is tender. Poppers can also be cooked on a grill.

Sara Mast, Elkhart Lake, WI
Loretta Newswanger, Orrstown, PA

Fire-Roasted Pickle Wraps

Bacon strips
Pickle, whole
Cream cheese, softened

Push one end of bacon strip onto sharp stick. Thread pickle onto stick. Wrap bacon around pickle and secure end on top of stick. Poke toothpicks into bacon to secure to pickle if needed. Roast slowly over fire until bacon is done and pickle blisters. Dip into cream cheese before eating.

DORETTA MAST, LaGrange, IN

Biscuit on a Stick

Open can of refrigerated biscuit dough. Flatten each biscuit by hand and wrap around cooking stick. Hold over hot coals to bake.

Fruit on a Stick

Firm fruits like large chunks of pineapple or whole apples or peaches can be cooked on a stick. Prepare a dip for eating them with.

Baked Apple on a Stick

Push sharp stick about halfway through bottom of apple. Hold apple above hot coals, rotating stick occasionally until apple cracks on all sides. Carefully remove skin from apple with sharp knife. Adult should help children do this. Now comes the fun part! With apple still on stick, roll it in cinnamon-sugar mixture until evenly coated.

Fannie Stoltzfus, Christiana, PA

Curly Twists

1 stick butter, softened
2 to 3 cans refrigerated biscuits
Cinnamon-sugar mixture

With buttered hands, roll biscuit dough into long rope. Wrap rope of dough around stick or dowel rod in coil fashion. Bake over open fire coals until nicely browned and baked through. Pull off stick carefully and roll in cinnamon-sugar mixture.

Carolyn Lambright, LaGrange, IN

WOOFERS

2 cans crescent roll dough
Cream cheese filling
Fruit pie filling

Preheat end of bamboo stick. Wrap one triangular section of crescent dough around end of stick, making sure bottom and sides of dough are tightly sealed and create a cone about 6 inches long. Bake over campfire, turning constantly until nicely browned and baked through. Remove dough from stick, fill with cream cheese filling, and top with fruit pie filling.

CREAM CHEESE FILLING:

16 ounces cream cheese
½ cup maple syrup or powdered sugar
Stevia to taste (optional)
1 teaspoon vanilla

Beat together cream cheese, maple syrup, stevia, and vanilla until smooth. Transfer to cake-decorating bag or plastic bag with small hole cut in bottom corner to make filling cones easier.

Note: These can also be made in a pie iron. Grease pie iron. Put piece of crescent dough on each side of pie iron and fill with cream cheese filling and pie filling. Close pie iron and bake over campfire coals until dough is done. The filling for these will be heated through, unlike in the cones.

KATHRYN K. KAUFFMAN, Myerstown, PA

Traditional S'mores

Large marshmallows
Graham crackers
Hershey's chocolate bars, divided

Toast 2 marshmallows over fire until brown and puffy. Break graham cracker in half. Place piece of chocolate on one half. Top with toasted marshmallows and other half of graham cracker. Press lightly together.

EMMA BYLER, New Wilmington, PA

Peanut Butter S'mores

Large marshmallows
Graham crackers

Hershey's chocolate
bars, divided
Peanut butter

Toast 2 marshmallows over fire until brown and puffy. Break graham cracker in half. Place piece of chocolate on one half. Top with toasted marshmallows. On other half of graham cracker, spread peanut butter. Place on top of marshmallows. Press lightly together.

Emma Byler, New Wilmington, PA
Katieann J. Gingerich, Howard, OH
Emeline Girod, Salem, IN

Strawberry-Cream Cheese S'mores

Large marshmallows
Graham crackers
Hershey's chocolate
bars, divided

Cream cheese, softened
Fresh strawberries, sliced

Toast 1 to 2 marshmallows over fire until brown. Break graham cracker in half. Place piece of chocolate on one half. Top with toasted marshmallow(s). On other half of graham cracker, spread cream cheese and top with slices of strawberries. Sandwich two sides together, pressing lightly.

Emma Byler, New Wilmington, PA

Campfire S'mores

Large marshmallows
Graham crackers

Chocolate bars, divided,
or peanut butter cups
Fresh strawberries, sliced

Toast marshmallow on stick over fire until brown and puffy. Sandwich marshmallow between graham crackers with strawberry slices and piece of chocolate or peanut butter cup.

Miriam Coblentz, Greenfield, OH

Ritz S'mores

Large marshmallows   **Peanut butter cups**
Ritz crackers

Toast marshmallow on stick over campfire until brown and puffy. Sandwich marshmallow between 2 Ritz crackers with a peanut butter cup.

Mrs. Sheryl Byler, Vestaburg, MI

We make Ritz s'mores using traditional Hershey's candy bars.
Anna Byler, Spartansburg, PA
Esther D. Schwartz, Harrisville, PA

S'mores Variations

- For the peanut butter lover, spread peanut butter on graham cracker or use peanut butter cup.
- Use fudge-striped cookies to replace graham crackers and chocolate.
- Use Ritz crackers and mint patties in place of graham crackers and chocolate.
- Try other candy bars in place of chocolate (Hershey's cookies and cream, Mr. Good Bar, Rolo caramel chocolates, etc.)

Ellen Miller, Dowling, MI

- Use Ritz crackers in place of graham crackers.

Fannie K. Swarey, Charlotte Courthouse, VA

- Use thin slices of apple in place of graham crackers.

Becky Fisher, Lancaster, PA

- Add slices of strawberries and/or bananas to traditional s'mores.
- Giant marshmallows are fun to toast for s'mores.

Fannie S. Byler, New Wilmington, PA

- In a pinch, use chocolate chips in place of candy bar.

Elizabeth Yoder, Kenton, OH

STUFFED MARSHMALLOWS

Make a slit in marshmallow and stuff some chocolate chips inside before toasting. Makes a yummy chocolaty treat that is fun for children.

LINDA FISHER, Ronks, PA

STRAW HATS

| Ritz crackers | Large marshmallows |
| Peanut butter | Chocolate chips |

Spread peanut butter on cracker. Toast marshmallow on stick and place on top of peanut butter with chocolate chips. A very good snack.

LIZZIE ANN SWARTZENTRUBER, Newcomerstown, OH

Cooking in a Pie Iron

Those who work hard eat hearty!

AMISH PROVERB

A pie iron is a great campfire tool designed to cook food directly in the coals of the fire. It has two sides with a cavity for holding food so that the food is fully contained within. The best pie irons are made of cast iron and have long metal rods with wooden handles. Square pie irons are nice as they fit the shape of sliced bread, but circular pie irons can work as a crimp to seal in contents when using bread.

With a little imagination, you can cook a wide variety of things in a pie iron. Also, children love to fill them and can successfully cook their own food with a little supervision. And no matter if you call the pies hobo pies, moon pies, mountain pies, or pudgy pies, the results are delicious!

To use a pie iron, you need a fire that has burned down to hot coals. So start fire 45 to 60 minutes before cooking. Generally pie irons should be preheated before filling. You will also need a platform or table that will withstand the hot pie iron.

Pie Iron Care

- When finished using pie iron, wash and dry it thoroughly. Then spray both sides with cooking spray and place paper towel between the two sides. It won't rust when stored like this.

Elizabeth Stoltzfus, Quarryville, PA

- To clean pie iron, scrub with stainless steel scrubber (chore ball), warm water, and dish soap. Dry with dark-colored towel. Place on hot stovetop or grill and heat until fully dry. To prevent rusting, use paper towel to rub lard over the inside and outside of iron while still hot. The lard keeps them from rusting.

Mrs. David (Malinda) Kanagy, Mifflintown, PA
Mrs. Aaron M. Miller, Marion Center, PA

- Save silica gel packs that come in packages and place them inside camping cookware like pie irons and dutch ovens to help prevent moisture from creating rust during storage.

COOKING in a PIE IRON

Sunday Morning ~~Chaos~~ Breakfast

1 cheery, well-started campfire
1 table
1 bucket warm, soapy water with rag
Chairs
Mountain pie irons
10 children and 2 adults
1 pitcher pancake batter
Scrambled eggs
Sausage, fried and cut in pieces
Bacon, fried and crumbled
Maple syrup
Butter

First, settle children's squabbles over who gets which chair while preheating pie irons. Dash inside for forgotten plates and spoons. Give toddler a piece of bacon.

Next, supervise hot pie irons while children brush them with butter and pile in eggs and meat. Grab rag to wipe up spilled pancake batter, then pour batter over eggs and meat yourself.

Send children to Daddy with filled and closed pie irons for toasting over hot coals. Feed baby.

After children have one mountain pie each, join Daddy at table to fill your own pie iron. Hand baby to middle son. Ask oldest son to bake your mountain pie. Clean up spilled meat and wipe maple syrup jar. Help younger children make their second round of mountain pies.

Finally, savor your perfectly baked mountain pie. Inhale the fresh, dewy air. Take crying baby from middle son. Quickly finish eating before feeding baby again.

Once all tummies are filled, send children to gather dishes and leftover food. Thank God for the beautiful morning, for your precious, noisy family, and for His merciful provision.

RACHEL STOLTZFUS, Paradise, PA

CAMPFIRE EGGS AND BACON

1 egg
1 pinch salt
1 pinch pepper
2 tablespoons diced ham (optional)
3 to 4 slices bacon

Beat egg and pour into one side of greased pie iron. Sprinkle with salt and pepper. Add ham. Close iron and hold steady over hot coals, then turn for even cooking. Egg is done when it solidifies. Drape bacon over metal ends of skewer and hold over fire until slightly crisp.

LORANN M. LEID, Ephrata, PA

BREAKFAST HOBO PIES

1 loaf bread, sliced
10 eggs
Salt and pepper to taste
1½ pounds sausage
Cheese, sliced or shredded

In skillet, scramble eggs and season with salt and pepper. Chop finely and set aside to cool. Brown sausage in skillet and chop finely; drain and cool. Heat pie irons over campfire, then butter both inside cavities. Put slice of bread then cheese on each side. Top cheese with sausage and eggs. Close pie iron. Hold over campfire coals until golden brown on both sides.

RHODA BYLER, Brookville, PA

We add cooked bacon and call them "mountain pies."
AMANDA BYLER, Curwensville, PA

We like to put bacon strips and small sausage patties on the grill to cook, and we suggest serving these pies with salsa or ketchup.
MRS. DAVID (MALINDA) KANAGY, Mifflintown, PA

We like to use the little sausage patties in these.
DORETTA MAST, LaGrange, IN

Bacon and Cheese Mountain Pie

Butter, softened
Bread slices

Cheese slices
Fried bacon

Butter bread slices on one side. Place one bread slice butter side down in preheated pie iron. Top with cheese slice and 2 to 4 slices of bacon. Top with second bread slice butter side up. Close pie iron. Place over campfire coals until golden brown on both sides.

Marcus Zook, Newbury, PA

Breakfast Sandwiches

Bagels
Precooked eggs
Salt and pepper to taste

American cheese
Canadian bacon
Fresh spinach (optional)

Set bottom half of bagel in pie iron. Top with egg and season with salt and pepper. Layer on cheese (don't let it hang over edge or hole in middle), bacon, and spinach. Top with other half of bagel. Close pie iron and place in hot coals until bagel has browned nicely and cheese is melted.

Rebecca Yoder, Venango, PA

Pie Iron Pancake Breakfast Sandwich

PANCAKE BATTER:

3 eggs, separated
9 tablespoons
  butter, melted
3 tablespoons sugar
2¼ cups milk

3 cups flour
2 teaspoons salt
6 teaspoons baking
  powder

In mixing bowl, mix egg yolks, butter, and sugar. Add milk, flour, salt, and baking powder, mixing well. Beat in egg whites.

TOPPINGS:

Scrambled eggs
Bacon, sausage,
  and/or ham, cooked
  and chopped
Onions, diced
Peppers, diced

Cheese, shredded
Potatoes, cooked and
  diced or sliced
Maple syrup or gravy
  for serving

Preparation: Preheat and grease pie iron. Pour in approximately ¼ cup pancake batter, or enough to cover bottom of one side of pie iron. Fill with desired toppings. Pour thin layer of pancake batter on top. Do not overfill as pancake batter will rise while cooking. Quickly close pie iron and keep it level. Bake over hot coals until browned on both sides. Serve with maple syrup or gravy.

Note: Biscuit dough may be used in place of pancake batter. Press biscuit dough into both sides of pie iron. Put filling on top of one side of dough, close pie iron, and bake over coals.

KATHRYN K. KAUFFMAN, Myerstown, PA
MARCUS ZOOK, Newbury, PA

Stuffed French Toast

4 eggs
½ cup milk
½ teaspoon salt
½ teaspoon vanilla
½ teaspoon cinnamon
Spray oil or butter

1 loaf bread, sliced
8 ounces cream cheese, softened
Fresh fruit, chopped, or pie filling

In bowl beat eggs, milk, salt, vanilla, and cinnamon. Preheat pie iron and grease with spray or butter. Dip one side of bread slice in egg mixture and put it egg side down into pie iron. Spread cream cheese on bread and top with 3 tablespoons or more of fruit. Put second dipped bread slice egg side up on top. Close pie iron and heat on hot coals to toast both sides. Serve with maple syrup and/or ice cream.

ROSELLA HOCHSTETLER, New Holstein, WI

Applesauce Pancakes

1 cup Bisquick baking mix
½ teaspoon cinnamon
1 egg

½ cup applesauce
½ teaspoon lemon juice
¼ cup milk

In bowl combine all ingredients, stirring well. Grease preheated pie iron and fill one side with batter. Close and lock pie iron. Hold level while cooking on warm coals. Don't turn pie iron until you have peeked inside to see that batter has thickened up nicely. Cook until both sides are brown. Serve with syrup.

EMMA BYLER, New Wilmington, PA

Barbecue Chicken Wrap

¼ cup cooked,
  chopped chicken
1 tablespoon
  shredded cheese
Barbecue sauce

Honey mustard
Chopped onions
Chopped peppers
1 large tortilla

Mix chicken and cheese. Stir in barbecue sauce, honey mustard, onions, and peppers to your taste. Place mixture on tortilla and fold up. Place in pie iron and close. Heat in campfire coals until lightly browned.

Martha Mast, North Bloomfield, OH

Chicken-Bacon-Ranch Pies

2 pounds ground chicken
Bacon bits
Ham, chopped
Ranch dressing

Shredded cheese
Bread slices
Butter

In frying pan, fry chicken in grease, stirring to crumble. Add bacon bits and ham in quantities that suit your taste. Add ranch dressing to create a creamy coating. Meat mixture shouldn't be dry. Fold in cheese to your taste. Place buttered bread slice in greased pie iron, butter side down. Add a generous scoop of meat mixture. Top with second slice of buttered bread butter side up. Close pie iron and toast over hot coals until bread is lightly browned.

Mary Chupp, Nappanee, IN

TASTY TACOS

12 (5-inch) corn tortillas	1 ounce taco seasoning
1 pound ground beef, browned	1 cup shredded cheese
	½ cup chopped onions

Mix beef with taco seasoning. Lay one tortilla in greased pie iron and top with beef, cheese, and onion. Top with second tortilla. Wet edges slightly where they will come together. Close pie iron. Cut off any excess tortilla on outside. Cook in campfire coals until slightly browned.

MARTHA MAST, North Bloomfield, OH

PIE IRON TACO BAKE

FILLING:

1 pound ground beef or bulk sausage	Toppings of choice (onions, peppers, cheese, etc.)
1½ cups pizza sauce	Sour cream
½ teaspoon salt	Chopped lettuce
¼ teaspoon pepper	

Brown beef in skillet. Add pizza sauce, salt, and pepper (omit salt and pepper if using sausage).

CORN BREAD:

1 cup cornmeal	½ teaspoon salt
1 cup flour	1 egg
2 tablespoons honey	4 teaspoons baking powder
¼ cup butter	
1 cup milk	

Mix all ingredients together in batter bowl with pour spout.

Preparation: Preheat and grease pie iron. Pour approximately ¼ cup corn bread batter into one side of pie iron. Scoop desired amount of meat mixture onto batter. Top with toppings of choice, then pour thin layer of corn bread batter over top. Quickly close pie iron and hold level. Bake over hot coals until nicely browned on both sides. Serve with sour cream and lettuce if desired.

KATHRYN K. KAUFFMAN, Myerstown, PA

Chili Tortilla Mountain Pie

2 small tortillas
1½ tablespoons chili
1 teaspoon salsa

2 tablespoons
    shredded cheese

Lay one tortilla in greased pie iron and top with chili, salsa, and cheese. Top with second tortilla. Wet edges slightly where they will come together. Close pie iron. Cut off any excess tortilla on the outside. Cook in campfire coals until slightly browned.

Martha Mast, North Bloomfield, OH

Chicken Quesadilla Pie

Butter
2 slices bread
Chicken, cooked
    and diced

Thickened teriyaki sauce
    or sauce of your choice
Shredded cheddar
Shredded mozzarella

Preheat pie iron over hot coals. Place buttered bread slice butter side down in pie iron. Mix chicken and teriyaki sauce and spoon onto bread. Sprinkle with cheddar and mozzarella. Top with buttered bread slice butter side up. Close iron and heat in hot coals until bread is toasted.

Enos and Maria Wickey, Monroe, IN

Philly Cheesesteak Hobos

Refrigerated french
    bread dough
Deli roast beef

Cheese slices
Onion, sliced
Green pepper, sliced

Coat inside of preheated pie iron with cooking spray. Cut 2 pieces of dough to fit in iron. Sandwich beef, cheese, onion, and green pepper between dough pieces. Close iron and put in hot coals until bread is toasty brown.

Tena Byler, Wilcox, PA
Rhoda Byler, Brookville, PA

Grilled Cheese Pie

Butter
2 slices bread
Seasoned salt

2 cheese slices
Ham, bacon, or other
   meat of choice (optional)

Preheat pie iron over hot coals. Generously butter bread slices and sprinkle with seasoned salt. Lay bread buttered side down in pie iron cavities. Top each bread slice with cheese slice. Place meat on top of cheese. Close iron and heat in hot coals until bread is toasted.

ENOS AND MARIA WICKEY, Monroe, IN

Tuna Melt Mountain Pie

Bread slices
Tuna or chicken salad

Cheese slices

Put 3 tablespoons tuna salad and cheese slice between 2 slices of bread. Place in greased pie iron. Cook in coals until toasted to your liking.

MARTHA MAST, North Bloomfield, OH

Pie Iron Sandwiches

Bread
Salad dressing (like
  Miracle Whip)
Italian seasoning
Oregano

Salt and pepper
Thin-sliced deli meat
Cheese slices
Tomato, sliced
Lettuce

Spread 2 bread slices with salad dressing. Sprinkle with Italian seasoning, oregano, salt, and pepper to taste. Layer with slices of meat, cheese, tomato, and lettuce. Close in greased pie iron and toast until lightly browned.

BARBARA BRENNEMAN, Fredonia, PA
TOBIAS AND RACHEL HERTZLER, Charlotte Courthouse, VA

Pizza Mountain Pies

Butter
Bread slices
American or provolone
  cheese slices

Ground beef or sausage,
  cooked, or chipped ham
Pepperoni (optional)
Pizza sauce

Preheat pie iron over hot fire. Generously butter 2 bread slices. Lay buttered side down against pie iron (one slice in each section of iron). Top each bread slice with cheese slice. Then top one slice with warm ground beef and 1 tablespoon pizza sauce. Close pie iron and heat in hot coals until toasted on both sides.

Sylvia Renno, Jackson, OH
Mrs. David (Malinda) Kanagy, Mifflintown, PA

We replace the cheese slices with an 8-ounce package of cream cheese, ½ cup sugar, and 1 egg blended together.
Albert and Amanda Byler, Clarks Mills, PA

These are "Pizza Hobos" at our house.
Mrs. Levi Mast, Apple Creek, OH

We call these "Pizza Pudgies." We spread pizza sauce on both sides of the bread and layer on our favorite toppings.
Sara Mast, Elkhart Lake, WI

PIZZA PIES

Refrigerated pizza dough	Shredded cheese
Pizza sauce	Other toppings of choice
Pepperoni slices	

Preheat pie iron and spray with cooking oil. Fit piece of flattened pizza dough into iron and load with sauce, pepperoni, cheese, and other toppings of choice. Top with another piece of flattened dough to cover contents. Close pie iron and trim off excess dough. Hold over hot coals until dough is toasty brown. Flip and check often so pizza pie doesn't burn. Slide pie out of iron. Let cool. Be careful as filling will be hot.

LYDIA HOSTETLER, Brookville, PA

HOBO PIZZA SANDWICHES

2 pounds ham, chopped	½ green pepper, sliced
2 (4 ounce) cans	1 pint pizza sauce
mushrooms, drained	2 cups shredded cheese
½ onion, chopped	Bread, sliced

Mix ham, mushrooms, onion, pepper, pizza sauce, and cheese. Spread scoop of mixture on bread slice and place in preheated and greased pie iron. Top with second slice of bread. Close pie iron. Toast over campfire coals until both sides are browned.

EMMA MILLER, Ashland, OH

Jalapeño Popper Pies

1 cup crushed cornflakes
¼ teaspoon salt
¼ teaspoon pepper
¼ teaspoon garlic powder
Cooking spray or
  melted butter

4 slices whole
  wheat bread
8 ounces cream
  cheese, softened
4 cheddar cheese slices
2 jalapeño peppers

Grease pie iron. Crush cornflakes in bowl and stir in salt, pepper, and garlic powder. Coat bread slice with cooking spray or melted butter on one side and dip into cornflake crumbs. Set coated side down on pie iron. Spread with thick layer of cream cheese. Top with cheddar slice. Slice jalapeño peppers, removing the seeds. Place slices of one pepper on cheese and top with another cheese slice. Spread cream cheese on second bread slice, then coat opposite side with cooking spray or butter and dip into cornflakes. Lay bread cream cheese side down on cheddar slice. Close pie iron and toast over coals until both sides are nicely browned. Makes 2 pies.

EMMA BYLER, New Wilmington, PA

Stuffed Portobello Bake

1 large portobello
  mushroom
Mayonnaise
Onion
Tiny cooked salad shrimp

Fresh basil leaf
Shredded cheese
Breadcrumbs
Olive oil

Remove stem and gills from mushroom. Spread mayonnaise inside cap. Top with onion and shrimp. Add basil leaf, whole or shredded. Top with a handful of cheese, some breadcrumbs, and a drizzle of olive oil. Set in pie iron and close. Bake level in hot coals, without turning over, until breadcrumbs are toasted. Absolutely delicious!

REBECCA YODER, Venango, PA

CREAM CHEESE CAKES

1 yellow cake mix	1 cup sugar
8 ounces cream cheese	3 cups pie filling

Mix cake according to package directions. In another bowl, mix cream cheese and sugar. Coat pie irons with cooking spray. Spoon cake batter into one side of pie iron until bottom is almost covered. Dollop with cream cheese and pie filling. Fill rest of pie iron with cake batter. Fasten pie iron closed, but don't tilt it. Hold level over fire for a couple of minutes to bake cake batter until browned. Flip pie iron and bake other side till browned. Serve warm with ice cream.

MRS. JONI LILLIE HOSTETLER, Edinboro, PA

CINNAMON CAKES

1 yellow cake mix
1 cup brown sugar
3 teaspoons cinnamon

Prepare cake mix according to package directions. In another bowl, mix cinnamon and sugar. Spray pie irons well. Fill one side of pie iron with cake batter until almost full. Sprinkle with cinnamon-sugar mixture and slightly mix into batter. Fasten pie iron closed, but don't tilt it. Hold level over fire for a couple of minutes to bake and brown cake batter. Flip to other side to bake until browned. Serve warm with ice cream.

MRS. JONI LILLIE HOSTETLER, Edinboro, PA

Fruit Cakes

1 can buttermilk biscuits
1 (8 ounce) package cream cheese
Pie filling of choice

Flatten a couple of biscuits. Put one in greased pie iron. Top with cream cheese, pie filling, and second flattened biscuit. Close pie iron. Hold over coals, turning at least once, until biscuits are baked and lightly browned.

Mrs. Miller, Fredericksburg, OH

Dessert Mountain Pies

1 package cake or brownie mix	1 (8 ounce) tub whipped topping
1 (8 ounce) package cream cheese, softened	½ cup sugar Pie filling or thickened fruit

Prepare cake mix as directed on box. In separate bowl, blend cream cheese, whipped topping, and sugar until smooth. Grease preheated pie irons. Spoon ¼ to ½ cup cake batter into one side of each pie iron. Close and bake over hot campfire coals. Remove cake from iron and top with cream cheese mixture and pie filling.

Mrs. Roman (Alma) Yoder, Patriot, OH

Campfire Strawberry Shortcakes

Angel food cake, sliced 1 inch thick
Fresh strawberries, sliced
White baking chips

Coat preheated pie iron with cooking spray. Lay one slice of cake in iron and top with strawberries, white baking chips, and second slice of cake. Close pie iron and hold over hot coals for a few minutes, rotating iron. These bake fast, so check often until lightly toasted.

Tena Byler, Wilcox, PA

Other fruits, such as raspberries, also work.
Karen Mast, LaGrange, IN

Dream Pies

Refrigerated flaky biscuit dough
Melted butter
Cinnamon-sugar mixture
Lemon pie filling

Flatten biscuit and brush with melted butter, coating well. Sprinkle with cinnamon-sugar mixture. Press into pie iron and spread with pie filling. Top with second biscuit prepared as the first. Press edges together. Close pie iron and bake on warm coals. Turn every 2 minutes until biscuit is browned and firm to the touch. Takes 5 to 8 minutes total. Garnish as desired but tastes great plain.

Emma Byler, New Wilmington, PA

Apple Cream Mountain Pies

8 ounces cream cheese, softened	1 teaspoon cinnamon
½ cup sugar, divided	8 slices bread
1 teaspoon vanilla	Butter, softened
	1 pint apple pie filling

In mixing bowl, whip cream cheese, ¼ cup sugar, and vanilla until smooth. In small bowl, mix ¼ cup sugar and cinnamon. Preheat pie iron over campfire. Spread butter on one side of bread slices and sprinkle with cinnamon-sugar mixture. Place butter side down in pie iron. Spread with 2 heaping tablespoons pie filling, and top with 1 tablespoon cream cheese mixture. Place second slice of bread with butter and cinnamon-sugar facing up. Close pie iron and heat over coals until bread is toasted. Makes a good dessert while camping.

Note: You can also use strawberry or blueberry pie filling; just omit cinnamon.

MRS. DAVID (MALINDA) KANAGY, Mifflintown, PA

Toasted Dessert Sandwiches

Bread slices	Cream cheese, softened
Butter	Cherry pie filling

Spread butter on one side of bread and cream cheese on the other. Put bread butter side down in pie iron and spoon pie filling on top of cream cheese. Cover with bread slice butter side up. Close pie iron and bake in hot coals. Turn over after 2 to 3 minutes, and check after 4 to 5 minutes. When bread is well toasted, remove. Filling will be hot.

EMMA BYLER, New Wilmington, PA

We call these "Pudgy Pies."
KERI BARKMAN, Napp, IN

We call these "Moon Pies."
MRS. LEVI MAST, Apple Creek, OH

PBJ Mountain Pies

Bread	Jelly
Butter	Powdered sugar
Peanut butter	

Butter bread slice and place butter side down in pie iron. Spread with peanut butter and jelly. Top with second buttered bread slice butter side up. Close pie iron. Hold over campfire coals until golden brown on both sides. Roll in or dust with powdered sugar while still warm.

Amanda Byler, Curwensville, PA

Banana–Peanut Butter Pie

Butter	1 banana
2 slices bread	1 chocolate candy bar
Crunchy peanut butter	

Preheat pie iron over hot coals. Spread butter on one side of each slice of bread and peanut butter on opposite side. Lay buttered side against pie iron (1 slice in each section of iron). Thinly slice banana and place over peanut butter. Break up candy bar and layer over banana. Close iron and place in hot coals until bread is toasted. Check often so it doesn't burn. Delicious!

Enos and Maria Wickey, Monroe, IN

S'mores Pie

2 slices bread	Mini marshmallows
Peanut butter	Fresh fruit, sliced
Chocolate chips	(optional)

In preheated pie iron coated with cooking spray, place bread slice spread with peanut butter. Place chocolate chips and marshmallows on peanut butter. Spread peanut butter on second bread slice and lay it facedown over marshmallows. Close pie iron and toast pie over campfire coals.

LIZ BRICKER, Middlefield, OH
BECKY FISHER, Lancaster, PA
DEHLIA WENGERD, Willshire, OH

Cinnamon S'more Mountain Pies

Bread, sliced	Hershey's milk
Butter, softened	chocolate bars
Cinnamon	Marshmallows

Preheat pie iron and coat with cooking spray. Spread butter on slice of bread and sprinkle with cinnamon. Place butter side up in pie iron. Cover with chocolate pieces (I cover nearly the whole slice with chocolate). Put 4 marshmallows on top. Butter second bread slice and sprinkle with cinnamon. Place buttered side on marshmallows. Close pie iron. Hold over coals until golden brown on both sides. Optional: Place pie iron on grill that is at least 350 degrees and flip at least once.

MRS. DAVID (MALINDA) KANAGY, Mifflintown, PA

Marshmallow Bread

Bread slices	**Cream cheese, softened**
Peanut butter	**5 to 6 marshmallows**

In greased and preheated pie iron, place bread slice spread with peanut butter. Spread cream cheese on second bread slice and set aside. Toast marshmallows on stick over campfire coals. Place marshmallows on peanut butter and top with cream cheese slice. Close pie iron and toast over campfire coals.

BECKY FISHER, Lancaster, PA

Cooking in Foil Packets

*If you cannot have something,
make the best of what you have.*

ANNA A. SLABAUGH, APPLE CREEK, OH

Aluminum foil is an inexpensive and universal tool for cooking on a campfire grate, down in campfire coals, or on a grill. A popular trend has been to use foil to create a tight packet around the ingredients in which steam from their own juices helps to cook the food.

In this section, you will also find some recipes that recommend an aluminum pan on a grill. These pans can be a great way to cook and have easy cleanup.

We recommend using heavy-duty aluminum foil for outdoor cooking, and often you will want to spray it with oil to prevent food from sticking. But if you prefer that your ingredients not touch the foil directly, you can place a sheet of parchment paper between the foil and the food.

When cooking foil packets over a campfire, build the fire 45 to 60 minutes before you are ready to cook so that you have a hot bed of coals to place the packet in.

COOKING in FOIL PACKETS

Campfire Hard-Boiled Eggs

This recipe doesn't use foil, but instead an inexpensive paper cup placed down in campfire coals similarly to a foil packet. Once campfire has burned down to only hot coals, place paper cup (no foam or plastic) with water in coals. Place whole raw egg in its shell in water and watch it boil. It is amazing that the water boils and the cup won't burn up until the water is all boiled away.

MRS. SUSIE MAST, Bear Lake, MI

Cheese Soufflé

8 slices bread	6 eggs
¼ cup butter	2 cups milk
Smokies or ham	½ tablespoon onion salt
1 pound cheese, cubed	½ teaspoon salt
or shredded	Pinch pepper

Cube bread into well-greased 9x13-inch aluminum pan. Add butter, smokies, and cheese. In bowl, mix together eggs, milk, onion salt, salt, and pepper. Pour over bread. Refrigerate overnight. Set pan on hot grill and close lid. Stir every 10 to 15 minutes until done.

JOLENE BONTRAGER, Goshen, IN

Chicken, Bacon, and Ranch Grillatillas

Ranch dressing	Bacon, fried and
Flour tortillas	crumbled
Chicken, grilled	Shredded cheddar
and diced	

On each tortilla, spread small amount of ranch dressing and place on sheet of aluminum foil. Pile on one half of tortilla desired amount of chicken, bacon, and cheese, then fold over other half. Wrap foil to enclose tortilla. Lay on hot grill. Cook each side 3 to 5 minutes until grill marks appear on tortilla and cheese is melted. Serve dipped in additional ranch dressing.

EMMA BYLER, New Wilmington, PA
RUTH BYLER, Quaker City, OH
MALINDA M. GINGERICH, Spartansburg, PA
LIZZIE ANN L. KURTZ, New Wilmington, PA

Grilled Ham and Cheese Sandwich Loaf

1 loaf Italian bread
4 tablespoons butter

½ to ⅔ pound cooked
  ham, thinly sliced
3 slices swiss cheese,
  cut in half

Slice about two-thirds of the way through bread loaf and cut 12 equal slices. On every other slice, spread butter and tuck in a slice each of ham and cheese, dividing evenly to create 6 sandwiches. Gently press loaf together and place in center of large sheet of heavy-duty aluminum foil sprayed with oil. Fold foil and seal edges. Grill over medium heat 15 to 20 minutes until cheese melts, rotating loaf for even heating. Remove from grill and open carefully. Pull apart sandwiches. Serves 4 to 6.

REUBEN AND WILMA SCHWARTZ, Conneautville, PA

Chicken Subs

6 sub buns
Ranch dressing
Salad dressing
American cheese slices
3 pounds chicken
  breasts, grilled

Baby swiss cheese slices
Onion, sliced
Lettuce leaves
Tomatoes, sliced

Heat grill to 350 degrees. Spread ranch dressing on top sides of buns and salad dressing on bottom sides. Place American cheese on salad dressing, then chicken, swiss cheese, and onion. Sandwich sub together and wrap in foil. Warm on grill only long enough to melt cheese. Serve with lettuce and tomatoes.

JERRY AND MARY HERTZLER, Charlotte Hall, MD

Hot Dog Toppings

When grilling hot dogs, slice green peppers and onions into strips and place on sheet of foil greased generously with butter. Grill for a few minutes and use as hot dog topping for extra tastiness.

Malinda M. Gingerich, Spartansburg, PA

Onions on the Grill

3 large onions, sliced
2 tablespoons honey
½ teaspoon salt
½ teaspoon ground mustard

In large bowl, combine all ingredients, tossing to coat. Place on double thickness of heavy-duty aluminum foil (about 18 inches square). Fold over and seal edges. Place on grill, covered, over medium heat for 20 to 25 minutes, turning once, until onions are tender.

Barbara Brenneman, Fredonia, PA

Grilled Cabbage

Cabbage (1½-pound head), cut in wedges or slices
¼ cup chopped onion
½ teaspoon garlic salt
¼ teaspoon pepper
⅓ cup butter, softened

Place cabbage on large sheet of aluminum foil (double thick). Sprinkle with onion, garlic salt, and pepper. Dab soft butter all over cabbage. Close and seal packet. Cover with second large sheet of aluminum foil and seal edges. Place on hot grill and cook until tender throughout. Takes approximately 20 minutes.

Emma Byler, New Wilmington, PA
Malinda M. Gingerich, Spartansburg, PA

Baked Beans

1 (1 pound, 15 ounce) can
  great northern beans
Bacon, chopped, or
  hot dogs, sliced
¼ cup chopped onion

¼ cup ketchup
2 teaspoons mustard
¼ scant cup brown sugar
½ teaspoon chili powder

Mix all ingredients and place in foil roasting pan. Cover with foil for most of cooking time. Place on hot grill (around 350 degrees) and cook until heated through and liquids have thickened. Rotate a few times for even heating.

Abner and Rachel Zook, Bellerville, PA

Grill Baked Potatoes

Scrub potatoes and leave skins on. Dry with towel. Rub butter on skins and place on individual sheets of foil. Add salt, pepper, seasoned salt, or other seasonings to taste. Wrap foil around each potato tightly. Heat grill to 350 degrees and cook potatoes 40 to 50 minutes, turning at least once. Serve with butter, sour cream, or your favorite dressings. It is also good with barbecued chicken.

Esther D. Schwartz, Harrisville, PA

Stuffed Potatoes

6 large potatoes	**½ teaspoon seasoned salt**
½ cup sour cream	**¼ teaspoon pepper**
½ cup shredded cheese	**Parsley flakes**

Wrap each whole potato individually in foil and bake until tender on grill or in firepit. Cut potatoes in half and scoop out centers. Mash centers with potato masher and mix with sour cream, cheese, seasoned salt, and pepper. Fill potato shells and sprinkle with parsley. Wrap each half in foil and bake on grill or in firepit until heated through.

Note: These can also be started in your home kitchen. Bake potatoes in oven; then mix filling and fill them. Do final bake outdoors to heat before eating.

Naomi Swarey, Mechanicsville, MD

Potato Wedges

Peel and cut potatoes into wedges. Mix some flour with seasonings of choice. Dip potatoes in melted butter and roll in seasoned flour. Spray large sheet of heavy-duty aluminum foil with cooking spray and wrap potatoes in foil, sealing edges. Cook on embers of campfire or on hot grill until tender.

IDA BYLER, Frazersburg, OH

Cheesy Campfire Potatoes

1½ pounds potatoes, cut into ⅛-inch slices
½ cup chopped onion
4 tablespoons butter, melted
¼ teaspoon seasoned salt
¼ teaspoon pepper
¾ cup shredded mozzarella
¾ cup shredded cheddar
¼ cup grated parmesan

Let campfire burn down to hot coals. In bowl, toss together potatoes, onion, melted butter, seasoned salt, and pepper. Layer several sheets of aluminum foil together in large square. In center of square, place half of potato mixture and top with mozzarella, cheddar, and parmesan. Put remaining potato mixture on top of cheese. Fold foil together to cover all and seal edges. Place on grill rack over hot coals. Flip packet often so cheese doesn't burn. Cook potatoes until tender, about 30 to 40 minutes. Serves 3 to 4.

MALINDA M. GINGERICH, Spartansburg, PA

We add a half pound of cooked and crumbled bacon and some minced chives to this recipe. We also save half of the mozzarella and cheddar to sprinkle on just before serving.
JANET WEAVER, Lititz, PA

Grilled Taters

Potatoes, scrubbed
½ cup butter
2 tablespoons
  parsley flakes

1 teaspoon salt
½ teaspoon pepper
½ teaspoon garlic salt
½ teaspoon seasoned salt

Cut potatoes into 1-inch cubes. Melt butter and add parsley, salt, pepper, garlic salt, and seasoned salt. Add potatoes and stir until well coated. Spoon onto sheet of aluminum foil and wrap foil to enclose potatoes. Preheat grill to 400 degrees. Place packet on hot grill for 10 to 15 minutes or until potatoes are tender soft. Delicious served with ranch dressing, barbecue sauce, or ketchup.

Mrs. Rachel Yoder, Homer, MI
Rebecca Muller, Dundee, OH

BACON-POTATO BUNDLES

4 large potatoes,
   peeled and cubed
4 slices bacon

Salt and pepper
Butter

Place potatoes on large sheet of heavy-duty aluminum foil. Dot with butter. Cut bacon into bite-sized pieces and place on top. Sprinkle with salt and pepper. Fold foil over and seal edges. Place on grill and cook until potatoes are tender.

MRS. DAVID LAMBRIGHT, Mount Vernon, OH

CHILI-CHEESE FRIES

1 bag frozen french fries
Chili, any variety
Shredded cheddar

Bacon, fried and
   crumbled
Green onions, chopped

Spray large sheet of heavy-duty aluminum foil with cooking spray. Dump frozen french fries in center and spread into single layer. Spread chili over top and sprinkle with cheddar, bacon, and onions. Fold and seal foil tightly around fries. Set packet directly in hot coals for 20 to 25 minutes or until cheese is melted and fries are soft and hot.

TENA BYLER, Wilcox, PA

CAMPFIRE SWEET POTATOES

Wrap whole sweet potatoes in heavy-duty aluminum foil and place in hot coals for about 30 minutes until soft. Cooking time will depend on size of potatoes. Can also be cooked on grill.

RACHEL MILLER, Millersburg, OH

Campfire Potatoes

5 medium potatoes,
  peeled and thinly sliced
1 medium onion, sliced
6 tablespoons butter
⅓ cup shredded cheese
2 tablespoons minced
  fresh parsley
1 tablespoon
  Worcestershire sauce
Salt and pepper to taste
½ to ⅓ cup chicken broth
6 slices bacon (optional)

Place potatoes and onion on large piece of heavy-duty aluminum foil (about 20 x 30 inches). Dot potatoes with butter. In bowl, combine cheese, parsley, Worcestershire sauce, salt, and pepper. Sprinkle over potatoes. Top with bacon, if desired. Fold up foil around potatoes then add broth. Seal edges of foil well. Grill covered over medium coals 35 to 40 minutes until potatoes are tender.

LIZZIE ANN SWARTZENTRUBER, Newcomerstown, OH
SUSIE KING, Allenwood, PA
SALLY MULLET, Kensington, OH
MRS. ROSEMARY YODER, Burke, NY

Put potatoes and onions in cast-iron skillet. Combine cheese, parsley, Worcestershire sauce, salt, and pepper; sprinkle over potatoes and toss to coat. Dot with butter and add broth. Cook over campfire coals until tender.
RUTH BYLER, Quaker City, OH

Zucchini Surprise

1 zucchini
4 ounces cream cheese
½ pint sour cream

Hamburger, sausage,
  or bacon, cooked
Salt to taste

Cut zucchini lengthwise. Scrape out the inside, creating a trough. Mix cream cheese and sour cream. Add hamburger. Spread inside zucchini. Sprinkle with salt. Wrap each half in sheet of aluminum foil (optional but will cook faster). Place on hot grill. Cook until zucchini is tender.

Mrs. Christina Schmidt, Salem, IN

BUNDLE OF VEGGIES

8 ounces whole, fresh
   mushrooms
8 ounces cherry tomatoes
1 cup sliced zucchini
1 tablespoon olive oil
1 tablespoon
   butter, melted

½ teaspoon salt
½ teaspoon onion powder
½ teaspoon Italian
   seasoning
⅛ teaspoon garlic powder
Dash pepper

Place mushrooms, tomatoes, and zucchini on a double thickness of heavy-duty aluminum foil (about 18 inches square). Combine olive oil, butter, salt, onion powder, Italian seasoning, garlic powder, and pepper. Drizzle over veggies. Fold foil over veggies and seal edges. Grill over medium heat 20 to 25 minutes or until tender. Substitute other vegetables of your choice if desired.

BARBARA BRENNEMAN, Fredonia, PA

CAULIFLOWER AND CARROT PACKS

1 small head cauliflower,
   cut into small florets
1 cup baby carrots,
   halved lengthwise
1 small onion, sliced

2 tablespoons olive oil
1 teaspoon garlic powder
½ teaspoon salt
½ teaspoon pepper

Combine all ingredients, stirring to coat vegetables well. Place mixture on oil-sprayed sheet of heavy-duty aluminum foil. Fold foil loosely so air can circulate, and seal edges tightly. Cook on grill over medium heat 15 minutes or until vegetables are tender, rotating once. Serves 4.

REUBEN AND WILMA SCHWARTZ, Conneautville, PA

CAMPFIRE BUNDLE

1 large sweet
  onion, sliced
1 large green pepper
1 large red pepper
1 large yellow pepper
4 medium potatoes, cut
  into ¼-inch slices
1 small head
  cabbage, sliced

6 medium carrots, cut
  into ¼-inch slices
2 medium tomatoes,
  chopped
1½ pounds smoked
  sausage, cut in
  ½-inch slices
½ cup butter, cubed
1 teaspoon salt
½ teaspoon pepper

Layer 3 large sheets of heavy-duty aluminum foil. Pile onion, peppers, potatoes, cabbage, carrots, and tomatoes. Place sausage on top and dot with butter. Sprinkle with salt and pepper. Fold foil around contents and seal tightly. Grill with lid closed over medium heat 30 minutes. Turn over and grill 30 minutes longer. Yields 6 servings.

KATIE M. BEILER, Parkesburg, PA

FOIL DINNERS

Potatoes, cubed small
Onions, chopped
Peppers, chopped

Ham, diced
Cheese, sliced
Salt and pepper

Have each person put their desired amounts of ingredients on sheets of heavy-duty aluminum foil sprayed with oil. Fold over and seal edges. Packets can be labeled with permanent marker with individual names. Place on grill or in hot campfire ashes to cook. Flip at least once. Cook until potatoes are tender.

MRS. SHERYL BYLER, Vestaburg, MI

We make these with Polish sausage and add carrots.
LIZZIE ANN L. KURTZ, New Wilmington, PA

Bratwurst Dinner

3 pounds bratwurst,
cut into thirds
1 pound baby carrots
2 jars whole mushrooms,
drained
1 large onion, sliced

3 pounds baby red
potatoes, cut
into wedges
2 tablespoons soy sauce
1 envelope onion
soup mix
1 teaspoon pepper
¼ cup butter

Mix bratwurst, carrots, mushrooms, onion, and potatoes. Place mixture on oil-sprayed, large sheet of heavy-duty aluminum foil. Pour soy sauce over top and sprinkle with onion soup mix and pepper. Dot with butter. Fold foil loosely so air can circulate, and seal edges tightly. Cook on grill over medium heat for about an hour or until vegetables are tender, rotating a few times. Alternative: Bake in oven at 400 degrees 1½ hours.

MIRIAM GINGERICH, Fredericksburg, OH

Grilled Potato and Hot Dog Packs

20 ounces potato wedges
4 hot dogs
1 small onion,
thickly sliced

¼ cup shredded cheddar
½ cup barbecue sauce

Divide potato wedges among 4 pieces of heavy-duty aluminum foil (about 18 inches square). Top each with hot dog, sliced onion, and cheese. Drizzle with barbecue sauce. Fold foil around mixture and seal tightly. Grill over medium heat 10 to 15 minutes or until heated through and potatoes are tender.

MRS. REUBEN N. BYLER, Dayton, PA

Grilled Chicken Pizza Packets

1 pound chicken breast,
  cut into 1-inch cubes
2 tablespoons oil
½ teaspoon oregano
½ teaspoon basil
¾ teaspoon salt
¼ teaspoon garlic powder
¼ teaspoon pepper

2 potatoes, thinly sliced
1 small onion,
  thinly sliced
16 pepperoni slices
1 cup chopped tomatoes
¾ cup shredded
  mozzarella
¼ cup grated parmesan

Mix chicken, oil, oregano, basil, salt, garlic powder, and pepper. Add potatoes, onion, and pepperoni. Divide mixture onto 4 (12-inch square) sheets of heavy-duty aluminum foil. Fold and seal edges. Place on hot grill and cook 18 minutes, turning over halfway through. Combine tomatoes, mozzarella, and parmesan. Open packets and sprinkle with tomato mixture. Grill 2 minutes.

Susan Byler, Mercer, PA

Turkey in a Hole

PREPARE THE HOLE:

Dig a hole 2 feet deep by 2 feet wide by 2 feet long for one turkey. Gather green saplings about 3 inches thick and 3 to 6 feet long. Cover the hole by laying saplings tightly together. You will need 3 to 4 full wheelbarrows of firewood. Wood scraps won't work. Build a fire on top of green saplings. It will take about 3 hours to burn through saplings and for fire to drip into hole.

PREPARE THE TURKEY:

1 whole turkey
3 sticks butter
Ice

Salt and pepper
Other seasonings
of choice

Tuck 1 stick butter under each leg and about half a stick under each wing. Fill turkey with ice cubes and sprinkle with salt and pepper and any other seasonings you'd like. Wrap turkey in 14 layers of heavy-duty aluminum foil, shiny side away from turkey. Optional: Wrap piece of wire fencing around aluminum-wrapped turkey so it is easier to grab ahold of when pulling it out of hole.

COOK THE TURKEY:

Scratch hole in ashes big enough for turkey to fit down into. Put prepared turkey in hole. Cover with red-hot coals. Then cover all completely with dirt so hardly any smoke comes out. Leave turkey in hole 7 to 8 hours.

This is very good eating and well worth the time it takes. The meat is very soft and moist. You'll be amazed.

RACHEL LANTZ, **Strasburg, PA**

GRILLED VENISON

½ cup butter, melted
Chopped garlic
Pepper
Garlic salt
Cilantro
Parsley
Cajun seasoning
Venison cubed steaks

2 medium onions, sliced
4 cups canned
  chopped tomatoes
Potatoes, sliced
Peppers, sliced
Carrots, sliced
½ cup butter
Garlic powder

In bowl, mix melted butter with garlic, pepper, garlic salt, cilantro, parsley, and Cajun seasoning. Baste venison steaks with mixture and grill until just done, then remove from heat. Make trough or packet of double layers of aluminum foil. Cut steak into bite-sized pieces and place on foil. Add onions, tomatoes, potatoes, peppers, and carrots. Dot with butter and season with garlic powder and additional pepper, garlic salt, cilantro, parsley, and Cajun seasoning as desired. Fold packet closed and seal edges of foil. Cook on grill for 1 hour or until vegetables are soft.

BARBARA BRENNEMAN, Fredonia, PA

GRILL STIR-FRY

1 pound shrimp, tails off
2 pounds fajita-style
  chicken strips (optional)
2 green peppers, sliced
2 onions, sliced

2 (8 ounce) boxes fresh
  mushrooms, sliced
1 pound spaghetti, cooked
Seasoned salt
Accent seasoning

Mix all ingredients together, seasoning to taste. Pour into aluminum foil roasting pan and place on grill heated to 250 degrees. Stir often until peppers and onions are tender. Delicious!

ELIZABETH SCHWARTZ, Carlisle, KY

Grilled Fish and Veggies

Butter	**Mini potatoes**
Peppers	**Fish fillets**
Onions (optional)	**Seasonings of your choice**
Carrots	**Lemon, thinly sliced**

Butter aluminum foil pan. Slice peppers, onions, carrots, and potatoes. Layer into pan. Top with fish fillets. Season as desired and dot with butter. Lay sliced lemon on top. Cover pan with foil. Grill about 1 hour over medium heat.

RAYMOND AND BARBI MILLER, Orwell, OH

Mayonnaise-Coated Grilled Fish

Spread mayonnaise on both sides of fish fillets and sprinkle with salt. Wrap in foil and place on grill. Delicious and very moist.

Rachel Lantz, Strasburg, PA

Grilled Fish

Fish fillets
Seasonings of choice
Salt and pepper to taste
Onion, sliced
Mushrooms, sliced (optional)
3 tablespoons butter, melted
½ teaspoon liquid smoke

Line baking sheet with heavy-duty aluminum foil. Place fish on foil and season to taste. Top with onion and mushrooms. Mix butter and liquid smoke and drizzle over top. Add more butter if needed to be sure fillets are all lightly coated. Place pan on grill, cover, and cook until fillets are flaky.

Rachel Bontrager, Burr Oak, MI

Southern Maryland Grilled Snakehead

Butter
Lemon juice
Snakehead fish fillets
Barbecue or Cajun seasoning

Heat grill to 250 to 300 degrees. Set foil or aluminum pie pan on grate. Put a pat of butter and dash of lemon juice on foil. Add single layer of fish fillets. Sprinkle with seasoning. Cook until done (180 degrees).

Note: Southern Maryland is well known for the sport of nighttime snakehead fishing. These are 25- to 30-inch fish.

Chris and Magdalena Swarey, Charlotte Hall, MD

Cheesy Grilled Bread

1 cup shredded cheddar
½ cup melted butter
1½ teaspoons paprika

1 teaspoon garlic powder
1 loaf french bread

Heat half of grill to medium heat. In bowl, combine cheddar, butter, paprika, and garlic powder. Slice bread into 2 halves lengthwise. Spread cheddar mixture evenly on both halves. Sandwich back together and wrap loaf in foil, folding and sealing edges. Cook on grill 15 to 20 minutes with indirect heat, turning to heat evenly. Slice to serve. Serves 6 to 8.

Variation: Substitute cream cheese for cheddar, and Italian seasoning for paprika.

REUBEN AND WILMA SCHWARTZ, Conneautville, PA

Grilled Garlic Bread

1 loaf french bread   ¾ teaspoon garlic powder
½ cup butter, softened

Slice bread into ½-inch portions, but don't cut through bottom crust. Combine butter and garlic powder and spread between slices and over top of loaf. Wrap in heavy-duty aluminum foil, sealing edges. Bake on grill rack 45 minutes to 1 hour, depending on temperature of coals. Serve hot. Serves 6 to 8.

FANNIE ANN BYLER, Reynoldsville, PA

Cheesy Campfire Bread

1 round loaf bread   1 tablespoon garlic
  (Hawaiian brand is best)   powder
1 stick butter   1 (8 ounce) bag shredded
                                  Colby-Jack cheese

Make slices into bread every 1 inch. Do not slice all the way through. Turn bread around and slice every 1 inch in opposite direction. Melt butter and mix with garlic powder. Pour into slices. Stuff cheese into each slice. Wrap loaf in aluminum foil. Place over low, indirect heat of campfire coals. When cheese is melted, it is ready to serve. Everyone just breaks off pieces to eat.

WILMA SCHWARTZ, Breman, IN

Smoked Cream Cheese

Set block of cream cheese in aluminum pie pan. Smoke cheese 45 minutes to 1 hour. Spread cream cheese out on plate and top with warm pepper jelly. You can also top cream cheese with your favorite seasoning before smoking. Serve with crackers.

BETTY SUE MILLER, Millersburg, OH

Grilled Chocolate Bananas

4 bananas, unpeeled   1 chocolate bar
4 tablespoons
   peanut butter

With sharp knife, slit through peel and banana lengthwise, though
not all the way through. Spread inside with peanut butter and place
2 squares chocolate in slit. Press closed. Wrap banana tightly with foil
and grill over hot coals for several minutes. Remove from foil and eat
with spoon, using peel for plate.

Mary Chupp, **Nappanee, IN**

*We make these by stuffing the bananas with mini
marshmallows and chocolate chips.*
Dehlia Wengerd, **Willshire, OH**

*These can be baked in an oven at 400 degrees for 8
minutes. Add chopped nuts for variation.*
Sarah Ann Miller, **Nashville, MI**

Grilled Apple Dessert

10 cups thinly sliced
   peeled apples
1 cup old-fashioned oats
1 cup packed
   brown sugar
¼ cup flour
3 teaspoons cinnamon
1 teaspoon nutmeg
   (optional)
¼ teaspoon ground
   cloves (optional)
¼ cup diced cold butter

Place apple slices on double-thick sheet of heavy-duty aluminum foil (about 12 x 24 inches). In small bowl, combine oats, brown sugar, flour, cinnamon, nutmeg, and cloves. Cut in butter until mixture is crumbly. Sprinkle over apples. Fold foil around apples and seal edges tightly. Place on grill, close lid, and grill over medium heat 20 to 25 minutes or until apples are tender. Serve warm with ice cream. Yields 6 servings.

LYDIA HOSTETLER, Brookville, PA

Berry Cobbler

1 cup crushed
   graham crackers
¼ cup packed
   brown sugar
⅓ cup flour
⅓ cup butter
6 cups fresh berries
   (blueberries,
raspberries,
blackberries, or
strawberries)
½ cup sugar
1 teaspoon cinnamon
2 tablespoons quick-
   cook tapioca
¼ teaspoon salt

In mixing bowl, combine graham crackers, brown sugar, and flour. Cut in butter and set aside. In second bowl, combine berries, sugar, cinnamon, tapioca, and salt. Set aside for 15 minutes, stirring occasionally. Place berry mixture in 9x13-inch disposable foil pan sprayed with oil. Cover with foil. Place on grill 5 inches away from medium heat for about 30 minutes. Rotate once. Remove foil covering and sprinkle with graham cracker mixture. Replace foil and grill 15 minutes longer. Serves 6.

REUBEN AND WILMA SCHWARTZ, Conneautville, PA

Campfire Cones

Waffle ice-cream cones	Mini marshmallows
Bananas, diced	Nuts, chopped
Fresh strawberries, diced	Other toppings as desired
Chocolate chips	

This is a great snack because there's no mess and you get to eat the bowl. Set out fillings in individual bowls for mix-and-match fun. Fill cone nearly full with your choice of fillings. Wrap cone with foil and set it on grill grate or lay in hot coals or ash for a few minutes until marshmallows are soft and chocolate is gooey. Unwrap and enjoy!

Fannie S. Byler, New Wilmington, PA
Fannie Stoltzfus, Christiana, PA

Tip: Put toppings in muffin pan so you don't have to deal with several small bowls.
Doretta Mast, LaGrange, IN

We like to fill cones with M&M's candies, peanut butter cups (miniature or cut up), mini marshmallows, and broken pretzels. We heat them on the grill.
Albert and Amanda Byler, Clarks Mills, PA

Baked Campfire Sweets

Batter of choice (brownie, corn bread, chocolate-chip cookie dough)

Place your favorite batter or dough in greased aluminum foil pie pan. Place another pie pan of equal size over top as lid. Use 3 to 4 wooden clothespins to hold together. Bake on grill rack above hot coals or directly on coals if not too hot.

My mom often did this when we were children, and we thought it was delicious. Now my children think the same thing.

Mary Chupp, Nappanee, IN

Cooking in Cast-Iron Skillets, Kettles, and Dutch Ovens

*When we climb the steep mountains of life,
we get a better view of the blessings.*

AMISH PROVERB

A platform fire is recommended for cooking directly on or over a campfire. Stack logs close together in at least three layers. Build the fire on top using tinder and kindling. As the fire burns down, the coals will develop a platform on which pots and skillets can be set directly, while the wood below continues to fuel the fire. Start this fire at least 45 minutes before cooking so the first layer of wood has turned to coals.

CARING FOR CAST IRON

- If food starts to stick to your cast-iron pans, grease them well with lard (no substitutes) and heat to a very high temperature in oven or on a burner. Do not leave unattended. You may need to repeat the process a few times. When washing cast-iron pans, always wipe them dry right away and set on stove until completely dry before putting away to keep them from rusting.

SARAH BYLER, **Knox, PA**

- Clean, dry, and grease cast-iron pans with lard. Never use cooking spray or oil. Place pan in ziplock bag until next use.

REBECCA YODER, **Venango, PA**

- Never wash cast-iron pans with soap of any kind. Wash in hot water only; then coat with oil.

LIZ BRICKER, **Middlefield, OH**

DUTCH OVEN

When cooking in a dutch oven, use a wooden spoon for stirring as metal spoons or whisks will scratch the surface.

MRS. GIDEON L. MILLER, **Loudonville, OH**

COOKING *in* CAST-IRON SKILLETS, KETTLES, *and* DUTCH OVENS

Open-Fire Biscuits

1 cup plus 2 tablespoons flour
1 teaspoon baking powder
½ teaspoon salt
¼ teaspoon baking soda

2 tablespoons lard or shortening
½ cup buttermilk
1 tablespoon lard or shortening

In mixing bowl, combine flour, baking powder, salt, and baking soda. Cut in 2 tablespoons lard with pastry blender or fork until grainy and coarse. Stir in buttermilk with fork. Do not overmix. Knead dough on floured surface a few times. Pat out dough to about ½ inch thick. Cut with floured biscuit cutter glass. Dough will get tough if handled too much.

Add 1 tablespoon lard (more if needed) to heavy cast-iron skillet or dutch oven and heat over hot coals or to around 500 degrees for about 7 minutes. Place biscuits in pan, turning once to coat with lard. Bake 10 minutes or until golden brown. A too-hot pan may result in doughy biscuits, so sometimes having the lid on makes for more even baking.

Mrs. Joel Peachey, West Columbia, WV

WILDERNESS BISCUITS

2 cups whole wheat flour	½ teaspoon cream of tartar
2 teaspoons sweetener of choice	½ cup cold butter
2 teaspoons baking powder	⅔ cup milk
½ teaspoon salt	1 egg

In bowl, blend flour, sweetener, baking powder, salt, and cream of tartar. Add butter and mix until crumbly. Stir in milk and egg. Form into balls about the size of walnuts. Bake in cast-iron skillet over campfire coals or on a grill 10 to 12 minutes until dough is firm and golden brown.

RUTH BYLER, Quaker City, OH

Good served with butter and honey or Campfire Stew.
SADIE BYLER, Frazeysburg, OH

CAMPFIRE DONUTS

Vegetable oil
Small tube biscuits
Powdered sugar or cinnamon-sugar mixture

Heat oil in cast-iron kettle over campfire until it reaches 350 degrees. Punch hole in each biscuit. Drop into hot oil. Watch carefully until donuts are browned. Remove from oil and drain on paper towel. Roll in powdered sugar or cinnamon-sugar mixture. Note: Use small biscuits as large ones will not get baked through before getting too brown on the outside. Eat while still warm.

MRS. LEVI MAST, Apple Creek, OH
DEHLIA WENGERD, Willshire, OH

Kids love to watch these donuts being made and love to eat them. Tip: Mix 1 cup sugar with 3 tablespoons cinnamon and keep in an air-tight container. Put some in empty shaker and shake over donuts instead of rolling them in cinnamon-sugar mixture. You can do the same with powdered sugar. Using a shaker keeps sugar from getting "dirty" from the donuts, and you keep the leftovers.
CAROLYN LAMBRIGHT, LaGrange, IN

Campfire Pancakes

2 eggs
2 cups buttermilk
  or sour milk
1 teaspoon lemon juice
1 teaspoon baking soda
4 tablespoons oil

2 tablespoons honey
1 teaspoon salt
2 cups spelt flour
2 teaspoons baking
  powder
Butter or coconut oil

Beat eggs and buttermilk together. Drizzle lemon juice over baking soda before adding to egg mixture along with oil, honey, and salt. Lastly, add flour and baking powder, stirring until just combined. Heat cast-iron skillet over campfire. Grease skillet and fry pancakes until lightly browned.

ESTHER TROYER, Walhonding, OH

Toasted Egg and Cheese Sandwiches

Butter
Eggs

Cheese slices
Bread slices

Put large cast-iron skillet on grill plate over fire. Melt butter in pan. Crack eggs (one per person) into pan. Fry until set, then flip. Top with cheese slice and bread slice. Flip when egg is done, and fry until bread is toasted.

MRS. SUSIE MAST, Bear Lake, MI

Quick and Easy Breakfast

6 slices bread, cubed
2 to 3 tablespoons butter
Ham, hot dog pieces, or
  other precooked meat

8 eggs
½ cup milk
Velveeta or American
  cheese slices

In cast-iron skillet, toast bread cubes in butter. Add ham. In bowl, beat together eggs and milk. Pour over bread. Place lid on skillet and heat until eggs are set. Remove from fire and top with cheese. Cover until cheese is melted.

ELLA ARLENE YODER, Arcola, IL

Forager's Breakfast Scramble

Meat of choice
Chives, chopped
Stinging nettle or kale,
  chopped finely
Dandelion blossoms
Onions, sliced
Peppers, sliced

Eggs, beaten and
  seasoned with salt
  and pepper
Tortillas
Salsa
Sour cream
Cheese

Place cast-iron skillet over hot coals and sauté meat. Add chives, nettle, dandelion, onions, and peppers, and cook until tender. Pour eggs over all and cook until set. Serve with tortillas topped with salsa, sour cream, and cheese.

RACHEL BONTRAGER, Burr Oak, MI

Breakfast Mix-Up

1 pound bacon, cut
  in 2-inch pieces
2 pounds hash browns
12 eggs, beaten
1 green pepper, diced

½ cup chopped onion
2 cans nacho cheese or
  cheddar cheese soup
1 pound precooked
  sausage

On grate over campfire coals, cook bacon in cast-iron skillet until well done. Place cooked bacon in 6-quart dutch oven sitting in hot coals. Reserve drippings. Fry hash browns in skillet, then place in dutch oven on top of bacon. Add reserved bacon drippings to skillet and scramble eggs along with pepper and onion. Spread one can of soup over potatoes. Heat sausage if needed and place on top of soup followed by scrambled eggs. Spread second can of soup over eggs then use large spoon to mix all ingredients. When heated through, serve with toast, salsa, and sour cream. Delicious!

TENA BYLER, Wilcox, PA
DEHLIA WENGERD, Willshire, OH

FAVORITE CAMPING BREAKFAST

¼ stick (4 ounces) butter
Diced onion
Diced green peppers

Shredded potatoes
(may use frozen)
Smoked sausage
Salt and pepper

Put butter in skillet. Add onion and green peppers, enough to suit your taste. Add potatoes. Cut sausage into 1-inch pieces and add to skillet. Add salt and pepper to taste. Fry over hot coals, stirring until done. We enjoy this with eggs over easy and toast on the side.

KATIE YODER, Sugarcreek, OH

CAMPFIRE OMELET IN A BAG

Eggs
Onion, chopped
Green pepper, chopped
Mushrooms, chopped
Ham, chopped
Sausage, fried and
   crumbled

Bacon, fried and
   crumbled
Cheese, shredded
Salt and pepper to taste
Ketchup
Salsa

Set large kettle half full of water over fire and bring to a boil. Gather 1 quart–sized ziplock freezer bag per person and line up additions and toppings in individual bowls. Crack desired number of eggs into each person's bag. Add desired additions of onion, green pepper, mushrooms, ham, sausage, bacon, and/or cheese. Season to taste. Seal bags, squeezing out all air. Have fun squishing bags between fingers to break eggs and combine ingredients. Put bags in boiling water for 13 to 15 minutes until eggs are set. Keep water boiling and don't let bags rest against side of kettle or bags will melt. Stir them with large wooden spoon. Serve with shredded cheese, ketchup, and salsa.

SUSAN BYLER, Mercer, PA

We love these. I've chopped Tater Tots and hot dogs to add to the eggs.
JERRY AND IDA PETERSHEIM, Kenton, OH

Campfire Breakfast for a Crowd

3 pounds bacon, cut up
4 pounds bulk
   sausage, fried
6 pounds little smokies
8 pounds Tater Tots
8 dozen eggs
1 (4 pound) box Velveeta
   cheese, cut into cubes

1 (16 ounce) container
   sour cream
Salt and pepper to taste
Additional seasonings
   of choice
75 to 100 tortillas
Salsa
Shredded cheese

In large kettle over hot coals, fry bacon until just done. Do not overdo and burn. Add sausage and smokies. Add Tater Tots and mix all together. Add eggs, and as they are beginning to set, mix in cubes of cheese. Add sour cream and season to taste. Serve immediately on tortillas with salsa and cheese. Feeds approximately 75.

L. Bontrager, Nappanee, IN

Country Brunch Skillet

6 strips bacon
6 cups cubed hash
  brown potatoes
¾ cup chopped
  green peppers

½ cup chopped onion
1 teaspoon salt
¼ teaspoon pepper
6 eggs, beaten
½ cup shredded cheddar

In cast-iron skillet over hot coals, fry bacon until crisp. Remove bacon from pan and fry potatoes in bacon grease until lightly browned. Add peppers, onion, salt, and pepper. Stir-fry until done. Pour eggs over top. Stir in cheese and cook until eggs set. Crumble bacon on top.

Mrs. Menno J. Miller, Gallipolis, OH

Suzy's Breakfast Special

Pizza dough of your choice	Sour cream
Eggs	Salsa
	Cheese

Roll pizza dough out to size of your cast-iron skillet. Over hot coals, scramble eggs in skillet. When done, set eggs aside. Clean skillet and spray with oil. Place pizza dough in skillet. Fry it a little, then flip and return to fire. Top with eggs, sour cream, salsa, and cheese. Add other toppings if you wish. Fry until dough is done and cheese is melted.

Tip: We have several 6-inch cast-iron skillets we use when camping. We premake the dough and roll it out into 6-inch circles, then put plastic wrap between circles and freeze. When camping, we let dough thaw overnight so that it is ready to make for breakfast.

RACHEL BONTRAGER, Burr Oak, MI

Breakfast Quesadilla

3 eggs	2 large tortillas
½ teaspoon salt	Shredded cheese
½ to ¾ cup fried sausage	

In frying pan, scramble eggs with salt. When almost done, add sausage and heat through. Lay tortilla on medium-hot grill with indirect heat, and sprinkle with cheese. Put egg mixture on top and sprinkle with more cheese. Put second tortilla on top. Grill until light brown; then gently turn quesadilla over and grill other side. Cheese helps to hold everything together, so use plenty.

ESTHER L. MILLER, Fredericktown, OH

Homemade Corn Bread

½ cup flour
½ cup sugar
2 teaspoons salt
½ teaspoon baking soda
1½ cups cornmeal
1 cup buttermilk
2 eggs, beaten
1 cup milk
2 tablespoons
   butter, melted

Grease 10-inch dutch oven. In large bowl, mix flour, sugar, salt, baking soda, and cornmeal. Add buttermilk and mix well. Wisk in eggs, milk, and butter until well blended. Pour batter into pot and cover with lid. Set dutch oven on ring of hot coals and place some coals on lid. Bake 35 to 45 minutes until done. Good served with campfire beans or chili.

Mrs. Gideon L. Miller, Loudonville, OH

Bacon-Fried Skillet Corn

8 ounces bacon, chopped
1 medium onion, chopped
2 medium green
   peppers, chopped
2 (16 ounce) packages
   frozen corn
1 teaspoon salt
½ teaspoon pepper

In large, deep cast-iron skillet on campfire grill rack over medium-high flame, cook bacon until evenly browned but still soft. Drain, reserving ⅓ cup bacon drippings. Return bacon and remaining drippings to skillet. Add onion and peppers and place over fire until tender. Stir in corn, salt, and pepper. Cook until corn is heated through and tender.

Malinda M. Gingerich, Spartansburg, PA

BACKYARD BEANS

1 (32 ounce) can
   pork and beans
1 (16 ounce) can
   kidney beans
1 (16 ounce) can
   butter beans
1 pound bacon, fried
   and crumbled
1 onion, chopped

½ cup bacon drippings
1 cup ketchup
1 cup brown sugar
1 tablespoon mustard
2 tablespoons
   Worcestershire sauce
1 can pineapple tidbits

Prepare fire. Mix all ingredients together in iron kettle or dutch oven. Cook over hot coals 45 to 50 minutes, stirring often. Serves 10 people.

IDA BYLER, Frazersburg, OH

Meat, such as hamburger, smokies, or chopped hot dogs, can be added to this.
MRS. DAVID RABER, Millersburg, OH

CHILI BAKE

2 pounds ground beef
1 quart corn, drained
1 (15 ounce) can
   chili beans
1 (15 ounce) can black
   beans, drained
1 cup chopped
   peppers (optional)

1 onion, chopped
1½ quarts salsa
¼ cup brown sugar
1 package taco seasoning
1½ cups cubed
   Velveeta cheese
Tortilla chips

In cast-iron pot over campfire, fry ground beef and drain off excess grease. Add corn, chili beans, black beans, peppers, onion, salsa, brown sugar, taco seasoning, and cheese. Simmer 10 minutes to blend flavors. Serve in bowls and scoop with tortilla chips to enjoy a very simple and light campfire dinner.

MARY CHUPP, Nappanee, IN

CAMPFIRE STEW

1½ quarts water
5 large potatoes, chopped
3 medium carrots, sliced
¼ head cabbage, chopped
½ cup diced celery
1 cup peas
1 cup green beans

2 large bell peppers, chopped
1 large onion, chopped
1 small zucchini, chopped
1 clove garlic, minced
1 to 2 pounds sausage, fried
Salt to taste

Heat water in cast-iron pot over campfire. Place potatoes, carrots, cabbage, celery, peas, and beans into boiling water and boil until they begin to soften. Add peppers, onion, zucchini, garlic, and sausage. Salt to taste. Boil uncovered. Add more water if too much evaporates. Ingredients can vary according to your taste and what is available. When ready, serve with hot bannock bread.

BARBARA BRENNEMAN, Fredonia, PA

Delicious served with Wilderness Biscuits.
SADIE BYLER, Frazeysburg, OH

We use 2 pounds of sausage and 2 pounds of bacon. I just guess on vegetable amounts and use whatever I have on hand or whatever is in season. Put in peas, cabbage, and broccoli last after other vegetables are soft, and just steam a few minutes so they don't get mushy. Lots of fresh garlic and oregano make this tasty. With a lid on the pot, it will cook quickly, but without lid, it can take an hour or more.
MARY CHUPP, Nappanee, IN

Bubble and Squeak

1 onion, diced	½ to 1 head cabbage
1 pound bulk sausage	⅓ cup vinegar
6 medium red potatoes, thinly sliced	Cheese (optional)

In large, deep skillet, sauté onion and sausage over hot coals. Add potatoes and move to fry over indirect heat until potatoes are halfway done. Add chopped cabbage and keep frying until cabbage is wilted and potatoes are done. Stir in vinegar. Cook a few minutes longer to blend flavors. Melt cheese on top if you wish.

Miriam Gingerich, Fredericksburg, OH

Neighborhood Cookout Stew

1½ pounds butter
20 pounds hamburger
5 quarts chopped onion
5 quarts chopped cabbage
5 quarts chopped
  potatoes
3 gallons water, divided

Seasoned salt to taste
5 quarts cubed carrots
5 quarts corn
5 quarts lima beans
5 quarts green beans
5 quarts peas
1 gallon kidney beans

Get a good fire going under 15-gallon cast-iron kettle. Put butter in kettle and melt to coat kettle. Add hamburger and onion, and fry until well browned. Add cabbage, potatoes, and 2 gallons water. Bring to a boil. Keep fire going so it continues to boil. Add seasoned salt to taste. Add remaining vegetables and more water as needed. Cook over slow fire for approximately 2 hours. Remove from fire when stew is done. Serve straight from kettle. Yields 240 1-cup servings.

EMMA BYLER, New Wilmington, PA

Fish Chowder

Pork or bacon, chopped
Fish, cut in slices
Onion, sliced

Potatoes, sliced
Salt and pepper
Biscuit dough (optional)

In dutch oven over hot coals, fry pork or bacon until fat renders. Lay single layer of fish slices on top of pork. Top with layer of onion and then potato. Season with salt and pepper. Add layer of biscuit dough rounds barely touching. Repeat layer of fish, onion, potato, seasoning, and biscuit dough until full. Cover with water and stew slowly for 30 minutes or until well done. Biscuit dough can be omitted if not wanted.

REBECCA HERSCHBERGER, Bear Lake, MI

Tenderloin Stew

Pork, venison, or
  beef tenderloin,
  cut into chunks
Vinegar
Potatoes, peeled
  and sliced
Carrots, sliced

Onions, sliced and
  separated into rings
Seasonings of choice
  (salt, garlic powder,
  seasoned salt, pepper,
  basil, onion salt, and/
  or poultry seasoning)
Butter

Soak tenderloin in water with splash of vinegar overnight. Drain. Heat large cast-iron kettle over campfire coals. Layer meat into pot with vegetables in between layers. After each layer, sprinkle with seasonings of choice. When pot is full, dot very generously with butter. The more butter you add, the tenderer it will be. Cook slowly over coals 2 to 3 hours or until meat is tender and vegetables are soft. Delicious and very satisfying.

RAYMOND AND MIRIAM TROYER, Blanchard, MI

Picadillo

Our standard campfire meal is made on a "disco" (a large agricultural disk with legs welded to it) with a fire built under it. We cube raw potatoes; chop onions, peppers, and garlic; add as much raw hamburger as desired; then fry all together. When nearly done, we lay corn tortillas on top to warm. Then we serve the mixture in tortillas with salsa.

BARBARA BRENNEMAN, Fredonia, PA
RUTH BYLER, Quaker City, OH

Venison Stew

4 cups venison or
   beef stock
1½ pounds venison,
   cut in 1-inch cubes
1 quart diced tomatoes,
   undrained
1 pound potatoes,
   chunked
1 pound carrots, chunked

1 medium onion, chopped
2 cups diced celery
1 cup dry navy beans
1 clove garlic, minced
½ teaspoon pepper
½ teaspoon salt
1 bay leaf

In 6-quart cast-iron kettle, combine all ingredients. Cover. Cook over well-maintained campfire coals 4 to 4½ hours, until all vegetables are tender. Remove and discard bay leaf.

Lovina Gingerich, Dalton, OH

Skillet Pizza

Pizza dough
Pizza sauce

Toppings of choice
(pepperoni, onion,
peppers, mushrooms,
cheese, etc.)

Place 2 cast-iron skillets over campfire coals to heat. Roll out about 1 cup pizza dough to size of your skillet. Remove 1 skillet from fire and spray with oil. Put dough in skillet and put back on grill rack over fire. Repeat steps with second skillet. Then remove first skillet and flip dough over. Top with sauce and toppings of your choice. Put skillet back on grate. Repeat steps with second skillet. Pizza is done when cheese is well melted and dough is lightly browned.

RACHEL BONTRAGER, Burr Oak, MI

Dutch Oven Pizza

Bisquick baking mix
Butter
1 cup pizza sauce

Toppings of choice
(pepperoni, green
peppers, onion,
mozzarella, etc.)

In firepit or charcoal grill, ignite 20 briquettes. Mix one batch 1 Bisquick biscuit dough according to package directions. Put generous amount of butter in preheated 10-inch cast-iron dutch oven with lid and spread to coat bottom and sides. Place dough in dutch oven and pat down level. Spread with pizza sauce and layer on toppings. Place lid on dutch oven. Set oven on 7 briquettes and lay 14 briquettes on top of lid. Bake 15 to 20 minutes before checking to see if pizza is done.

RAYMOND AND SUSAN GIROD, Salem, IN

Campfire Taco Salad

1 pound ground beef	Chili beans
1 package taco seasoning	Chopped lettuce
Shredded cheddar	Salsa
Chopped onions	8 snack-sized bags
Sour cream	nacho chips, crushed

In cast-iron skillet over campfire, fry ground beef and season with taco seasoning. Prepare bowls of cheese, onions, sour cream, beans, lettuce, and salsa. Give each person a bag of crushed nacho chips and let them pick toppings to add to bag. Eat straight from bag.

DEHLIA WENGERD, Willshire, OH
CAROLYN LAMBRIGHT, LaGrange, IN

Walking Tacos

1 pound lean ground beef or venison	1 cup frozen corn
2 (8 ounce) cans tomato sauce	1 (1.25 ounce) package chili seasoning mix
1 (15 ounce) can white kidney beans	12 snack-sized bags corn chips
	2 cups shredded cheddar

In large skillet in your home kitchen, brown beef then add tomato sauce, kidney beans, corn, and chili seasoning. Stir and bring to a boil. Cover skillet, reduce heat, and simmer 20 to 25 minutes. Later, in cast-iron kettle, bring chili to a boil over campfire, stirring as needed. Slightly crush bags of chips and cut tops off bags. Spoon 3 to 4 tablespoons chili into each one. Serve straight from bag with cheese on top. Chili can also be topped with salsa, lettuce, and/or chopped tomatoes.

BARBIE ESH, Paradise, PA

GRILLED RABBIT

1 rabbit, whole and cleaned	Salt
Worcestershire sauce	Seasonings of your choice

Brush rabbit with Worcestershire sauce and sprinkle with salt and any additional seasonings you prefer. Place on cast-iron grate over wood fire that is contained by blocks all around. Place heat-proof bowl over rabbit. Cook for several hours until meat is 165 degrees and pulling away from bone.

ELIZABETH K. SWAREY, **Charlotte Courthouse, VA**

DEEP-FRIED DANDELIONS

Dandelion blossoms	½ teaspoon baking powder
Peanut oil	½ cup flour
1 egg	¼ cup milk
½ teaspoon salt	2 tablespoons vegetable oil

Pick fresh dandelion blossoms. (Picking fresh just before frying means blossoms will stay open.) Rinse blossoms in salt water a few times. Fill heavy kettle halfway full with peanut oil and place over campfire coals to heat. In bowl, beat egg and add salt, baking powder, flour, milk, and vegetable oil. When peanut oil is hot, dip blossoms into batter and fry until golden brown.

My husband loves to fix these over the campfire.
SAMUEL AND SALOME EICHER, **Rockford, OH**

BROWNIE CAKE

1 (3.9 ounce) package
    instant chocolate
    pudding mix
1½ cups milk

1 (18.25 ounce) package
    chocolate cake mix
1½ cups chocolate chips

Line dutch oven with parchment paper. In bowl, whisk together pudding mix and milk until thickened. Stir in cake mix until well combined. Batter will be thick. Spread batter in lined dutch oven. Sprinkle evenly with chocolate chips. Cover pot with lid and set on ring of hot coals. Place about 17 hot coals on lid. Bake 30 to 40 minutes or until cake tests done with toothpick. Rotate pot and lid several times while baking. Let coals on lid burn down before replenishing a few. Very good served with ice cream.

MRS. GIDEON L. MILLER, Loudonville, OH

Chocolate Dumplings

1 egg
3 tablespoons butter
⅓ cup sugar
⅓ cup milk
1 teaspoon vanilla
1 cup sifted flour
2 teaspoons baking powder
1 teaspoon salt
2 tablespoons cocoa powder
3 tablespoons butter
⅓ cup brown sugar
1 tablespoon cocoa powder
Dash salt
2 cups water

In mixing bowl, beat egg and add 3 tablespoons butter, sugar, milk, and vanilla. Add sifted flour, baking powder, salt, and 2 tablespoons cocoa powder. Mix well; set aside. In cast-iron skillet on grate over hot coals, melt 3 tablespoons butter. Add brown sugar, 1 tablespoon cocoa powder, salt, and water. Stir until it boils. Remove from heat and drop tablespoonfuls of dough onto syrup. Cover with lid and simmer over fire 20 minutes. Serve with milk if desired.

Sylvia Renno, Jackson, OH

S'mores-wich

1 tablespoon butter
2 slices bread
1 milk chocolate bar or mini chocolate chips
1 whole graham cracker
4 large marshmallows

Butter 1 bread slice and place butter side down in cold skillet. Evenly space chocolate on unbuttered side of bread. Top with graham cracker. Cut marshmallows in half horizontally and place on cracker. Butter second bread slice and place butter side up. Heat skillet over medium-low heat of grill or on campfire until golden on bottom. Flip sandwich and cook until other side is golden. These can also be made in pie iron. I like to make ham and cheese sandwiches in pie iron for first course then serve these as dessert.

Lori Miller, Middlefield, OH

Honey Peach Crisp

6 peaches
¾ cup finely chopped
  pecans
1 tablespoon lemon juice
⅓ cup honey

½ cup flour
½ cup quick oats
¾ teaspoon cinnamon
⅓ cup butter, softened

Peel and slice peaches, arranging them in bottom of dutch oven. Sprinkle with pecans. In bowl combine lemon juice and honey, and pour over pecans. In second bowl, mix flour, oats, cinnamon, and butter until crumbly. Spread evenly over peaches. Cover dutch oven with lid and set on ring of hot coals. Place about 17 hot coals on lid. Bake 30 to 40 minutes, until peaches are tender and topping is browned. Rotate pot and lid several times while baking. Let coals on lid burn down before replenishing a few.

Keri Barkman, Napp, IN

Campfire Elephant Ears

Put large cast-iron skillet on grill plate over fire. Pour in cooking oil 1 inch deep. When oil is hot, deep-fry flour tortilla shells. Flip when they start to brown. Remove from oil when done and coat both sides with cinnamon-sugar mixture. Enjoy!

Doretta Mast, LaGrange, IN

Campfire Popcorn

Cut center out of big, round piece of firewood, creating an opening about 6 inches deep and wide. Place wood upright on fire or over hot ashes. Put butter and popcorn kernels in cast-iron skillet and set over hole in firewood. Cover with lid to keep popcorn from escaping, though it is fun to watch it pop.

LINDA FISHER, **Ronks, PA**

Skillet Popcorn

Cover bottom of cast-iron skillet with bacon grease or oil of choice. Put ½ to 1 cup popcorn kernels in skillet. Place skillet on grill grate over hot fire and watch kernels pop. This is exciting for children.

MARY STOLTZFUS, **Nottingham, PA**

Iced Meadow Tea

2 to 3 gallons water
1 handful fresh leaves each of spearmint,
**   peppermint, and balsam, washed**
2 to 3 cups sugar

Set kettle on tripod and add water. Bring water to a boil, then remove from heat. Stir in leaves. Cover tightly and let steep until nicely colored mint green, at least 2 hours. Strain and discard leaves. Stir in sugar. Allow to cool. Serve over ice.

You can also fill hot quart jars with tea, adding ¼ cup sugar to each quart. Refrigerate until ready to serve over ice.

Sylvia Renno, Jackson, OH

COOKING ON
A GRILL

*Sharing is such a simple way of
sweetening someone else's day.*

AMISH PROVERB

Grills fueled by charcoal, propane, or wood pellets have become the common way we cook outdoors in our modern era.

GETTING STARTED GRILLING

- Lightly coat grill grates with vegetable oil or cooking spray before preheating grill. Never spray vegetable oil directly over hot grill.
- If using gas/propane grill, preheat it to manufacturer's directions (10 to 20 minutes).
- If using charcoal grill, light about 50 briquettes before you begin meat preparation. When coals are coated with ash after 20 to 30 minutes, spread them evenly in single layer over fire grid. For medium-high heat grilling, wait 10 minutes after spreading out coals before grilling meat or other foods.
- To prevent sticking and to develop better grill marks, make sure to allow grill grid to preheat for at least 5 minutes before grilling.

ELIZABETH STOLTZFUS, Quarryville, PA

GETTING THE MOST FROM YOUR CHARCOAL

A charcoal grill will stay hot for 30 to 40 minutes before coals start to burn down. Utilize residual heat by grilling food such as chicken breasts and vegetables for the next day's dinner while grill is still hot.

ELIZABETH STOLTZFUS, Quarryville, PA

EASY GRILL CLEANUP

- Brush grill grates with oil or use nonstick cooking spray before heating to prevent food from sticking.

BARBARA DETWEILER, Quaker City, OH
DORA COBLENTZ, Greenfield, OH

- To keep meat from sticking to grill, cut an onion in half, pierce half with fork, dip in vegetable oil, and rub over hot grill. Not only does this keep meat from sticking to grill, but it also adds flavor.

EMMA MILLER, Ashland, OH
MRS. GIDEON L. MILLER, Loudonville, OH

- Set grill racks in the grass overnight. Dew helps release char, and it will come off easily in the morning.

RACHEL MILLER, Millersburg, OH

COOKING on a GRILL

Breakfast Biscuit Cups

Biscuit Mix:

8 cups flour
1 cup powdered milk
⅓ cup baking powder

8 teaspoons cream
 of tartar
2 teaspoons salt
1¾ cups shortening

Sift together flour, powdered milk, baking powder, cream of tartar, and salt. Cut in shortening. Pack loosely in air-tight container. To use: Combine 1 cup dry mix with ⅓ cup water. Bake at 450 degrees 10 to 12 minutes. Alternative: omit powdered milk and use milk instead of water to prepare.

Breakfast Biscuit Cups:

You will need several egg poaching cups or stainless steel measuring cups (1 cup size preferred). Prepare enough biscuit dough for your needs. Grease cups on outsides and bottoms. Spread a few tablespoons biscuit dough over greased cup. Use flour to keep dough from becoming too sticky. Place cup upside down on grill over hot coals to bake. After several minutes, remove cup from biscuit dough. It should come off easily; if it doesn't, wait a bit longer and try again. Turn biscuit cup right side up to finish baking. Fill cup with scrambled eggs and sausage or ham. Alternately, it can be filled with pie filling and topped with whipped cream for a dessert.

Rosella Hochstetler, New Holstein, WI

CREAMY BRUSCHETTA

French bread
Butter
½ cup mayonnaise
1 cup shredded
  mozzarella
1½ cups diced tomatoes

2 tablespoons parmesan
1 teaspoon oregano
¼ teaspoon basil
1 clove garlic, minced
Additional shredded
  mozzarella

Slice bread 1 inch thick. Butter each slice and place butter side down on pan or tray. Mix mayonnaise, mozzarella, tomatoes, parmesan, oregano, basil, and garlic. Place 1 scoop bruschetta mixture on each bread slice. Sprinkle with mozzarella. Preheat grill to 350 degrees. Grill bread until cheese is melted and bread is crispy.

BETTY SUE MILLER, Millersburg, OH

CHICKEN BLTS

1 to 2 chicken breasts
Italian dressing
1 pound bacon
4 sesame-seeded buns
Mayonnaise

Mustard
Cheddar, sliced
Lettuce
Tomato, sliced

Slice chicken and marinate in Italian dressing for 12 hours. Grill chicken and bacon until done. Spread buns with mayonnaise and mustard. Layer on chicken, bacon, and cheddar. Top with lettuce and tomato. Serves 4.

MRS. EDNA YODER, Mifflintown, PA

Chicken-Ranch Wraps

4 large flour tortillas
2 cups chopped,
   cooked chicken
¼ cup ranch dressing

½ cup shredded
   mozzarella
Oregano

Lay 1 tortilla on flat surface. Place ½ cup chicken, 1 tablespoon ranch dressing, 2 tablespoons mozzarella, and a sprinkle of oregano in center. Fold 4 sides of tortilla burrito-style. Spray with cooking spray. Grill over medium heat 1 to 2 minutes on each side, or until golden brown.

Janet Weaver, Lititz, PA

Grilled Chicken Tenders

1 cup butter
¼ cup salt
2 tablespoons garlic salt
¼ cup seasoned salt
4 cups water
3 cups white vinegar

1 cup apple cider vinegar
½ cup Worcestershire sauce
½ cup barbecue sauce
10 pounds chicken tenders

In saucepan, melt butter. Add salt, garlic salt, seasoned salt, water, white vinegar, apple cider vinegar, Worcestershire sauce, and barbecue sauce. Bring to a boil. Let cool 1 hour. Pour marinade over chicken tenders and let soak 24 hours. Drain and grill chicken over hot fire 3 to 5 minutes per side.

Susan Byler, Mercer, PA

Juicy Hamburgers

- For a juicier hamburger, add cold water to ground beef before grilling—½ cup water to 1 pound meat.

LIZZIE ANN SWARTZENTRUBER, Newcomerstown, OH

- For extra juicy and nutritious hamburgers, add ¼ cup evaporated milk per pound of meat before shaping it into patties.

DAVID AND LAURA BYLER, New Castle, PA

When grilling burgers, flip only once to retain juices.
LINDA FISHER, Ronks, PA

Grilled Burgers

2 pounds ground venison or beef	½ package saltine crackers, finely crushed, or ½ cup flax meal
2 teaspoons salt	
1 teaspoon pepper	
4 eggs	1 pound ground bacon (optional)
1 cup tomato juice	

Mix all ingredients thoroughly so they will hold together well on grill. Grease grill grates with butter. Grill burgers until done, flipping once. Overheating will dry out meat. Put in roasting pan and cover to let burgers steam.

MRS. JOEL PEACHEY, West Columbia, WV

Grilled Coffee Burgers

1 egg, beaten	¼ teaspoon garlic salt
¼ cup coffee	¼ teaspoon onion salt
¼ cup soda cracker crumbs	Dash pepper
¼ teaspoon oregano	1½ pounds ground beef
	½ pound ground sausage

In bowl, combine egg, coffee, cracker crumbs, oregano, garlic salt, onion salt, and pepper. Add beef and sausage and mix well. Form into patties and grill over firepit or on grill.

DEHLIA WENGERD, Willshire, OH

Bacon Cheeseburgers

1 pound ground beef
2 cups shredded cheddar
¼ cup Worcestershire
  sauce
½ cup chopped bacon,
  fried crisp
Salt and pepper to taste

In medium bowl, combine all ingredients and shape into 4 patties. Grill. Can also be done under broiler or baked on stone bar pan.

JERRY AND MARY HERTZLER, Charlotte Hall, MD

Deluxe Cheeseburgers

1 egg
1 (6 ounce) can
  tomato paste
1 tablespoon
  Worcestershire sauce
1 medium onion, chopped
½ teaspoon seasoned salt
½ teaspoon salt
⅛ teaspoon pepper
½ cup grated parmesan
  (optional)
½ teaspoon homemade
  seasoning mix*
2 pounds ground beef
8 slices cheddar

In large bowl, combine egg, tomato paste, Worcestershire sauce, onion, seasoned salt, salt, and pepper. Add parmesan and seasoning mix. Add ground beef and mix well. Shape into 8 patties and grill, covered, over medium heat 5 minutes on each side. Top each burger with cheese slice. Grill 1 to 2 minutes longer until cheese begins to melt.

*HOMEMADE SEASONING MIX:

¾ teaspoon Cajun
  seasoning
½ teaspoon garlic salt
1 teaspoon basil
1 teaspoon oregano
½ teaspoon paprika

Mix all ingredients together until well blended.

MENNO AND ESTHER YODER, Berlin, PA

BBQ Burgers

2 pounds ground beef
1 egg, beaten
½ cup quick oats
½ teaspoon onion salt

½ teaspoon garlic salt
¼ teaspoon pepper
¼ teaspoon salt
Barbecue sauce

In bowl, mix ground beef with egg, oats, onion salt, garlic salt, pepper, and salt. Shape into patties. Grill over hot coals, basting with barbecue sauce. Serve on buns with toppings of your choice.

These are truly a winner. We love them with Big Mac Sauce.
Susan Gingerich, Dalton, OH
Amanda Byler, Curwensville, PA
Katie M. Beiler, Parkesburg, PA
Lizzie Ann L. Kurtz, New Wilmington, PA

BARBECUED BURGERS

1½ pounds ground beef
1 egg, beaten
¼ teaspoon onion salt
¼ teaspoon garlic salt
¼ teaspoon pepper
⅛ teaspoon salt
¼ to ½ cup quick oats
Barbecue sauce*

In bowl, mix ground beef with egg, onion salt, garlic salt, pepper, salt, and enough oats to form patties. Shape into patties. Grill 6 to 8 minutes over medium heat, grill lid closed. Baste with barbecue sauce during last 5 minutes.

*BARBECUE SAUCE:

½ cup packed
   brown sugar
1 cup ketchup
⅓ cup sugar
¼ cup honey
¼ cup molasses
2 teaspoons mustard
1½ teaspoons
   Worcestershire sauce
⅛ teaspoon salt

In saucepan, combine all ingredients and bring to a boil. Remove from heat.

LIZZIE FISHER, Quarryville, PA

Just wait until you sink your teeth into these winning burgers. You'll agree they're something special.
ELIZABETH SHROCK, Jamestown, PA
REBECCA HERSCHBERGER, Bear Lake, MI

World's Best BBQ Burgers

¼ cup sauce*
⅓ cup quick oats
1 egg, beaten
¼ teaspoon onion salt
¼ teaspoon garlic salt
¼ teaspoon pepper
⅛ teaspoon salt
1½ pounds ground beef

In bowl, mix sauce with oats and egg. Add onion salt, garlic salt, pepper, and salt. Add ground beef, mix well, and form 6 patties. Grill over medium heat with grill lid closed 6 to 8 minutes. Baste with sauce while cooking.

*Sauce:

1 cup ketchup
½ cup packed
   brown sugar
⅓ cup sugar
¼ cup molasses or
   pancake syrup
⅓ cup honey
2 teaspoons mustard
1½ teaspoons
   Worcestershire sauce
¼ teaspoon salt
¼ teaspoon liquid smoke
⅛ teaspoon pepper
   (optional)

In saucepan, combine all ingredients and bring to a boil. Remove from heat.

Fannie Ann Byler, Reynoldsville, PA
Esther J. Gingerich, Fredericksburg, OH
Rosella Hochstetler, New Holstein, WI
Lydia Swarey, Charlotte Hall, MD
Miriam Zook, Gap PA

Chicken Burgers

4 large chicken breasts
2 eggs, beaten
1 sleeve Ritz crackers,
   crushed
Seasoned salt or
   seasonings of choice

Put chicken through grinder. Mix in eggs, crackers, and seasonings. Shape into patties and grill until done. Serve on hamburger buns with ranch dressing, sauce, ketchup, and/or cheese.

Elvesta Miller, Carrollton, OH

Homemade Pork Burgers

2 pounds ground sausage	½ onion, chopped, or ½
2 eggs	teaspoon onion powder
½ cup ground flaxseed	1 teaspoon garlic powder
½ cup almond milk	

Mix all ingredients together and form into patties. Put between sheets of waxed paper and freeze. Easy to grab for quick meal cooked on grill, over campfire, or in frying pan.

KEVIN MILLER FAMILY, Shipshewana, IN

Grilled Corn on the Cob

Leave husks on corn and soak in cold water 30 to 60 minutes. Place on hot grill until husks are black and corn is cooked. Turn a few times while cooking. May take 15 to 20 minutes. Remove husks carefully as they will be hot. Add butter and salt. Enjoy!

IDA BYLER, Frazersburg, OH
RACHEL MILLER, Millersburg, OH

We cut the tops off our corn (where the tassel is) and roast over medium to hot campfire coals for at least 10 minutes.
SYLVIA RENNO, Jackson, OH

We don't feel the need to soak corn in water before grilling.
MRS. CHESTER (ROSE) MILLER, Centerville, PA

Seasoned Grilled Corn

4 large ears sweet
corn in husks
¼ cup butter, softened

2 tablespoons minced
fresh parsley
¼ cup grated parmesan

Carefully peel back husk from each ear of corn to within 1 inch of bottom. Remove silk. In bowl, blend butter, parsley, and parmesan. Spread onto corn. Rewrap corn in husks and secure with butcher's string. Soak in cold water 20 minutes. Drain and place on grill over medium heat and cover. Cook 20 to 25 minutes or until tender, turning often. Serve with more parmesan. Yields 4 servings.

FANNIE S. BYLER, New Wilmington, PA

Grilled Asparagus

Asparagus spears　　**Farm Dust seasoning**
Oil　　　　　　　　　**Parmesan**

Put desired amount of asparagus in plastic bag. Add enough oil to coat well. Season with Farm Dust and parmesan. Grill over direct or indirect heat until soft tender.

Elizabeth Miller, Millersburg, OH

I like asparagus with Meadow Creek barbecue seasoning. Grilling doesn't take long.
Rachel Lantz, Strasburg, PA

Grilled Onions

Large candy onions
Seasoned salt
Barbecue sauce

Cut onions into ¼-inch slices. Sprinkle with seasoned salt and brush with barbecue sauce. Grill over hot grill to desired tenderness. These are very good served with steak or on top of grilled burgers.

Mrs. Sheryl Byler, Vestaburg, MI
Abner and Rachel Zook, Bellerville, PA

Baked Sweet Potatoes

Scrub sweet potatoes, dry, and poke holes in skin with fork. Grill 30 minutes to 1 hour at 400 degrees. Enjoy with your favorite toppings, such as butter, honey or brown sugar, and salt.

Betty Sue Miller, Millersburg, OH

Grilled Potato Wedges

4 medium potatoes
½ cup butter, melted
Salt and pepper or seasoning of choice

Cut each unpeeled potato into 4 wedges. Dip wedges in butter and place on hot grill over medium-high heat. Sprinkle with salt and pepper. Turn when potatoes are lightly browned. Cover grill and lower heat to medium low 10 to 15 minutes or until potatoes are soft. Serve with ketchup or ranch dressing. Any vegetables are good grilled like this, including asparagus, onions, and zucchini.

Ruby Ann Hochstetler, New Holstein, WI
Betty Byler, Brockway, PA

MINI GRILLED PIZZAS

DOUGH:

1 tablespoon yeast	⅛ teaspoon garlic salt
1½ tablespoons sugar	¼ teaspoon oregano
1 cup warm water	½ teaspoon salt
1½ tablespoons corn oil	2½ cups flour

Combine yeast, sugar, and water in mixing bowl. Let stand 5 minutes. Add remaining ingredients and mix together. Divide dough and roll out to your preferred size. Top with your favorite toppings. Preheat grill to 350 degrees. (We use a pizza stone.) Be sure to put plenty of flour on bottoms of your pizzas so they come off grill easily. Place pizzas on grill and cook until cheese is melted.

ELIZABETH MILLER, Millersburg, OH

We use this crust to make one large pizza on a grilling stone. We grill at around 400 degrees 10 to 15 minutes, rotating pan a couple of times while grilling.
REBECCA MULLER, Dundee, OH

TOPPINGS:

1 cup pizza sauce	Sliced mushrooms
½ pound ground beef, browned	Sliced black olives
Sliced banana peppers	4 cups shredded mozzarella
Chopped onions	

LIZZIE ANN SWARTZENTRUBER, Newcomerstown, OH

LESTER'S GRILLED PIZZA

1 tablespoon yeast
1 cup warm water
1 teaspoon sugar
1½ teaspoons salt
1 teaspoon Italian
  seasoning

¼ cup lard,
  shortening, or oil
3 cups flour (part whole
  wheat if desired)
Pizza sauce
Toppings of choice

Preheat charcoal grill. Use lots of charcoal and add a chunk of wood if desired. The goal is to get grill temperature as high as possible. After grill is ignited, place pizza stone on grill.

In mixing bowl, dissolve yeast in warm water. Add sugar, salt, Italian seasoning, lard, and flour, mixing well. Let rise briefly. Shape on very well-greased cookie sheet. Allow more time to rise if desired. Coat with sauce and top with your favorite toppings.

When grill reaches 600 degrees, slide pizza onto hot stone. Close grill lid. Check frequently. If grill is hot enough, pizza will be done in 4 to 8 minutes, depending on thickness of crust and amount of toppings. Remove from stone to serve.

This method results in a not-too-smoky crust that is extra delicious. I like to have a few crusts prepared for when the grill is hot. I grill them and keep them in the freezer.

ANNETTA MARTIN, Hamburg, PA

GRILLED BARBECUE PIZZA

- 1 (1.25 ounce) package active dry yeast
- 1 cup warm water
- 2 tablespoons oil
- 2 teaspoons sugar
- 1 teaspoon baking soda
- 1 teaspoon salt
- 2½ cups flour, divided
- 2 cups cubed grilled chicken
- ¾ cup barbecue sauce
- 2 cups shredded mozzarella

In mixing bowl, dissolve yeast in warm water. Add oil, sugar, baking soda, salt, and 2 cups flour. Mix well. Stir in enough remaining flour to form soft dough. Turn onto floured surface and knead 6 to 8 minutes until smooth and elastic. Cover and let rest 10 minutes. On floured surface, roll dough into 13-inch circle. Transfer to greased 12-inch pizza pan. Slightly build up edges of dough. Grill, covered, over medium heat 5 minutes. In bowl, combine chicken and barbecue sauce. Spread over crust. Sprinkle with cheese. Grill, covered, until crust is golden and cheese is melted.

FANNIE S. BYLER, New Wilmington, PA

Grilled Chicken–Bacon–Ranch Pizza

Dough:

1 tablespoon yeast
1½ tablespoons sugar
1⅓ cups warm water
1½ tablespoons oil
¼ teaspoon garlic salt

½ teaspoon oregano
2¾ cups flour
Cooking spray
Cornmeal

Dissolve yeast and sugar in warm water. Let sit 5 minutes. Add oil, garlic salt, oregano, and flour. Knead well to mix. Let rise until double in size. Spray 10x15-inch pizza pan with cooking spray. Sprinkle with cornmeal. Roll dough out and put on pan.

Toppings:

Ranch dressing
Mustard
4 cups shredded
  mozzarella
1 onion, sliced
½ pint mild banana
  pepper rings

Fresh mushrooms, sliced
1 chicken breast, sliced,
  grilled, and cut into
  1-inch pieces
½ pound bacon, fried
  and chopped

Spread ranch dressing and mustard on dough. Top with mozzarella. Layer with onion, pepper rings, mushrooms, chicken, and bacon. Let dough rise 15 minutes. Bake at 350 degrees on grill with lid closed or in outdoor oven for approximately 30 minutes until dough is done.

Mrs. Edna Yoder, Mifflintown, PA

Shish Kebabs

Chicken breast
Bacon
Cauliflower
Green peppers

Little smokies
Potatoes, cubed
  and cooked
Italian dressing

Cut chicken, bacon, cauliflower, and green peppers in bite-sized pieces and place in mixing bowl. Add smokies and potatoes. Coat with Italian dressing. Refrigerate overnight. Grill in shish kebab basket until meat is done and vegetables are tender.

MALINDA M. GINGERICH, Spartansburg, PA
MRS. DAVID LAMBRIGHT, Mount Vernon, OH

Kebabs

Chicken breast,
  sausage, or steak
Cherry tomatoes
Small mushrooms

Bell peppers
Onions
Zucchini
Italian dressing

Cut meat and vegetables into bite-sized pieces and place in air-tight container. Pour Italian dressing over all and refrigerate 12 hours. Soak bamboo skewers in cold water 20 minutes. Divide meat and vegetables on skewers. Keep pieces touching but loose enough for even grilling. Place on medium-hot grill. Turn every few minutes until all sides are browned. Brush a few times with Italian dressing while grilling. Meat should be juicy and vegetables crisp.

ABNER AND RACHEL ZOOK, Bellerville, PA
FANNIE K. SWAREY, Charlotte Courthouse, VA

Hawaiian Chicken Shish Kebabs

8 boneless, skinless
chicken breasts
2 large sweet onions

4 large green peppers
32 cherry tomatoes
2 cans pineapple chunks

Cut chicken into bite-sized pieces. Cut each onion into 16 wedges. Cut each pepper into 8 pieces. On 16 metal or soaked wooden skewers, alternately thread chicken, onion, peppers, tomatoes, and pineapple. Grill uncovered over medium heat 6 to 8 minutes or until chicken juices run clear. Serve with ranch dressing if desired.

Susie King, Allenwood, PA

Smoky Chicken Kebabs

3 slices bacon
4 teaspoons brown sugar
2 teaspoons seasoned salt
2 teaspoons paprika

1 teaspoon
Worcestershire sauce
1 teaspoon liquid smoke
2 large chicken breasts,
cut in 1-inch chunks

Chop bacon in food processor to create paste. Add brown sugar, seasoned salt, paprika, Worcestershire sauce, and liquid smoke. Mix. Use mixture to coat chicken. Refrigerate for 8 hours or overnight. Soak skewers in water 30 minutes before grilling. Thread chicken onto skewers. Grill over medium heat until cooked through. Takes about 30 minutes.

Janet Weaver, Lititz, PA

Grilled Pork Kebabs

12 small new red potatoes
¾ cup vegetable oil
¾ cup olive oil
⅓ cup lemon juice
⅓ cup Worcestershire
  sauce
¼ cup soy sauce
¼ cup white or
  red vinegar
3 tablespoons mustard
2 tablespoons minced
  fresh parsley
1 tablespoon pepper
2 cloves garlic, minced

2 (about 1 pound each)
  pork tenderloins, cut
  into 1½-inch cubes
6 frozen ears corn, cut
  in 2-inch sections
1 large onion, cut
  in wedges
1 large green pepper,
  cut in 1-inch pieces
8 ounces whole
  mushrooms
1 (20 ounce) can pineapple
  chunks, drained

Boil potatoes until just barely fork tender. Drain and rinse in cold water; set aside. In bowl, combine vegetable oil, olive oil, lemon juice, Worcestershire sauce, soy sauce, vinegar, mustard, parsley, pepper, and garlic. Divide mixture between 2 large ziplock bags. Put pork cubes in 1 bag and put corn, onion, green pepper, mushrooms, and pineapple in second bag. Marinate 3 hours. Drain and discard marinade. Thread meat, vegetables, and pineapple alternately on skewers. Grill over medium heat 8 to 10 minutes per side. Note: If using wooden skewers, soak them in cold water first so they don't burn.

Tena Byler, Wilcox, PA

Shrimp and Veggie Kebabs

1 cup Italian
  dressing, divided
2 pounds raw
  jumbo shrimp
2 large onions
16 cherry tomatoes
2 large green peppers,
  cut into 1½-inch pieces
16 large mushrooms

In large ziplock bag, combine ½ cup Italian dressing and shrimp. Cut each onion into 8 wedges. In another ziplock bag, combine onions, tomatoes, green peppers, and mushrooms with remaining salad dressing. Seal bags and turn to coat contents. Refrigerate 2 hours, turning occasionally to coat evenly. Drain and discard marinade. On 8 metal or soaked wooden skewers, alternately thread shrimp and vegetables. Grill kebabs, covered, over medium heat 3 minutes on both sides, or until shrimp turns fully pink. Yields 8 servings.

RHODA BYLER, Brookville, PA

In-a-Snap Steak and Veggie Kebabs

2 tablespoons Mrs.
  Dash original blend
1 pound beef sirloin, cut
  into 1½-inch chunks
2 cloves garlic, slivered
¼ red onion, cut
  into wedges
1 bell pepper, cut
  into wedges
8 cherry tomatoes
½ pound whole button
  mushrooms
Cooking spray
1 tablespoon olive oil

Sprinkle Mrs. Dash over beef, garlic, onion, pepper, tomatoes, and mushrooms and let sit 30 minutes. Heat grill to medium high. Spray 8 skewers with cooking spray and alternately skewer beef, garlic, onion, pepper, tomatoes, and mushrooms. Brush with olive oil and sprinkle with Mrs. Dash. Grill kebabs 6 to 10 minutes to desired doneness.

BARBARA DETWEILER, Quaker City, OH

Grill Basket Supper

Chicken breasts
Bacon
Fresh green beans,
 parboiled
Potatoes, parboiled

Carrots, parboiled
Onion
Peppers
Mushrooms

Cut up chicken, bacon, and vegetables into bite-sized chunks and mix together. Customize what you want to include and how much of each. Pour sauce over all and marinate in refrigerator for 1 day. When ready to grill, drain and place in grilling basket. Cook over grill or campfire until chicken and bacon are done and vegetables are tender.

Sauce:

¼ cup olive oil
¼ cup honey
⅓ cup soy sauce
2 tablespoons
 Worcestershire sauce

Garlic salt
Pepper
Parsley flakes

Mix all ingredients together.

Karen Mast, LaGrange, IN

GRILLED CHICKEN TIP

Before grilling chicken, cut it into uniform pieces or flatten breasts slightly for more even cooking. Coating chicken with a little oil or marinating before cooking will prevent moisture loss while grilling.

BARBARA DETWEILER, Quaker City, OH

EASY ITALIAN CHICKEN BREASTS

5 to 6 pounds chicken breasts
1 cup Italian dressing

Cover chicken with Italian dressing and marinate 6 hours or overnight. Remove chicken from dressing and reserve dressing. Grill chicken until done, basting with reserved dressing.

FANNIE ANN BYLER, Reynoldsville, PA

ITALIAN CHICKEN BREASTS

3 pounds chicken breasts
1 quart water
1 teaspoon baking soda
2 tablespoons salt

1 tablespoon apple cider vinegar
32 ounces Italian dressing
1 teaspoon Worcestershire sauce

Slice chicken breasts into equal portions. In large bowl, mix water, baking soda, salt, and vinegar. Add chicken to mixture. Add more water if chicken isn't completely covered. Cover bowl and refrigerate 12 hours. Drain and discard liquid. Mix Italian dressing and Worcestershire sauce. Pour over chicken. Cover bowl and refrigerate 12 hours. Drain and set aside. Grill chicken, taking care not to overcook. Place chicken in casserole dish and brush some of Italian dressing mixture onto chicken. Let chicken sit a few minutes before serving.

My husband thinks this chicken is tops!
FRIEDA EICHER, Clare, MI

Grilled Chicken with Sweet and Sour Sauce

10 pounds boneless, skinless chicken (breasts or thighs)	Italian dressing Meat tenderizer (optional)

Coat chicken generously with Italian dressing. Add meat tenderizer if desired. Chill 3 to 4 days, mixing pieces around a couple of times. Grill chicken until just done. Place chicken in roaster and cover with sauce.* Bake 2 hours at 200 degrees. Do not overbake as it can become dry.

*Sweet and Sour Sauce:

2 cups water	4 tablespoons salt
1¼ cups vinegar	2 pounds brown sugar
1 tablespoon Worcestershire sauce	⅓ cup Thermo-flo

In saucepan, place water, vinegar, Worcestershire sauce, salt, and brown sugar and bring to a boil. Thicken with Thermo-flo. We usually make a double batch and water bath can it to preserve it.

Emma Byler, New Wilmington, PA

Grilled Teriyaki Chicken

1 cup salad oil	1½ teaspoons chopped garlic
¾ cup soy sauce	Chicken breast fillets
½ cup brown sugar	
½ cup ginger ale	

In blender, mix salad oil, soy sauce, brown sugar, ginger ale, and garlic. Pour over chicken in shallow pan or ziplock bag. Use only enough to cover chicken. Remaining marinade can be saved for another time. Grill on preheated grill 5 to 7 minutes. Turn to finish. Don't overcook.

Abner and Rachel Zook, Bellerville, PA

Butterfield Grilled Chicken

1 (2 to 3 pound) whole chicken, rinsed
Olive oil
Salt and pepper

Cut chicken down backbone and lay flat. Tuck wings under and stick legs under skin at top of breast. Rub chicken with olive oil and sprinkle with salt and pepper. Grill on greased grate away from direct medium-hot heat 20 to 30 minutes per side. Keep grill cover closed. Chicken is done when juices run clear and internal temperature reaches 165 degrees. Cut into pieces and serve 4 to 6 people.

Bacon variation: Follow the above recipe, but stuff 4 to 5 bacon slices under chicken skin in as many places as possible.

REUBEN AND WILMA SCHWARTZ, Conneautville, PA

Bacon and Pepper Jack–Wrapped BBQ Wings

12 slices pepper
jack cheese
24 Tyson frozen
fully cooked honey
BBQ wings

24 slices thick-sliced
hickory-smoked bacon

Soak toothpicks in water for 1 hour to keep them from burning on grill. Cut cheese slices in half to form rectangles. Wrap piece of cheese around each wing. Wrap bacon slice around cheese to completely cover cheese. Secure with toothpicks. Grill over medium heat 13 to 15 minutes, turning occasionally to make sure all sides are crispy.

BARBARA DETWEILER, Quaker City, OH

Starr's Chicken on the Grill

½ gallon vinegar
1 quart vegetable oil
1 quart water
3 ounces salt
½ bottle Tabasco sauce
½ bottle Worcestershire
sauce

1 bottle beer (any kind)
1 quart tomato sauce
1 quart barbecue sauce
Chicken in pieces
Seasoned salt

Mix vinegar, oil, water, salt, Tabasco sauce, Worcestershire sauce, beer, tomato juice, and barbecue sauce. Cover chicken and soak for at least 1 full day. Put chicken on hot grill and sprinkle with seasoned salt. Brush with brine while cooking.

IDA BYLER, Frazersburg, OH

We call this "Charlie's Chicken."
AMANDA BYLER, Curwensville, PA

Grilled Chicken

Marinade:

2 cups vinegar
6 cups water
½ cup salt

2 ounces Worcestershire
sauce

Mix all ingredients together in large container.

2 to 5 whole chickens
Butter

Seasoned salt
Barbecue sauce

Cut up chickens into desired pieces and soak in marinade overnight. Add more water if needed to cover. Do not soak for longer than 18 to 20 hours or chicken will be too salty. Pound chicken with meat tenderizing hammer and grill over hot coals, turning frequently until browned and sizzling hot. Brush occasionally with melted butter and sprinkle with seasoned salt. Move chicken to roasting pan with a little water in bottom, cover, and bake at 350 degrees until internal temperature of 175 degrees is reached. Serve with barbecue sauce.

I like to use this chicken in casseroles and on pizza.
Mrs. Emanuel (Laura) Troyer, Blanchard, MI

Prize-Winning Pork Chops

Pork chops, approximately 1½ inches thick
Dry rub seasoning
Barbecue sauce

Apply dry rub to both sides of pork chops and refrigerate 30 minutes. Apply another coat of dry rub before grilling. When grill reaches 650 degrees, sear chops 2 to 3 minutes, then flip. After another 2 to 3 minutes, flip chops again and close top and bottom dampers of grill. Grill chops 3 to 4 minutes. Internal meat temperature should reach 170 degrees before removing. Serve with your favorite barbecue sauce. This recipe also works with steaks that are around 1½ inches thick.

ORPHA KEIM, Ashland, OH

Smoked Pork Loin

1 cup barbecue sauce
¾ cup brown sugar
1½ cups pineapple juice, divided
2 tablespoons mustard
1½ tablespoons seasoned salt
1 tablespoon lemon pepper
1 tablespoon fine black pepper
1½ teaspoons soy sauce
1 teaspoon Worcestershire sauce
1 teaspoon liquid smoke
7 to 10 pounds pork loin
Original Bearded Butcher Pork Rub
Weavers Smokehouse Meat Rub
Kosher salt

In bowl, mix barbecue sauce, brown sugar, ½ cup pineapple juice, mustard, seasoned salt, lemon pepper, pepper, soy sauce, Worcestershire sauce, and liquid smoke. Inject mixture into pork loin. You will have some left over. Rub loin generously with pork rub, smokehouse rub, and kosher salt. Preheat grill to 225 degrees. Smoke loin approximately 2 hours until internal temperature reaches 125 to 130 degrees. Mix leftover sauce with 1 cup pineapple juice and inject into loin. Wrap loin in heavy-duty aluminum foil and set on grill at 250 degrees and smoke until internal temperature reaches 147 degrees. Let meat rest off grill 10 minutes before slicing.

LEROY R. MILLER, *Big Prairie, OH*

Marinated Pork Chops

4 tablespoons soy sauce
3 tablespoons honey
1 tablespoon lemon juice
1 tablespoon olive oil
1 tablespoon garlic powder
½ teaspoon ground ginger
4 boneless pork chops

Combine soy sauce, honey, lemon juice, olive oil, garlic powder, and ginger. Add pork and turn to coat. Refrigerate 4 to 8 hours. Let meat warm to room temperature, then place on medium-hot grill and grill 6 to 8 minutes on each side. Let meat rest at least 5 minutes before serving.

NATHAN AND LAURA HOCHSTETLER, *Loudonville, OH*

Barbecued Ribs

2 pounds ribs
4 tablespoons honey
½ cup Italian dressing
½ cup barbecue sauce
4 teaspoons garlic powder
4 teaspoons onion powder
4 teaspoons Accent
4 teaspoons seasoned salt
2 teaspoons vinegar
12 ounces Mountain Dew
Barbecue sauce

Put ribs in cake pan. Mix honey, Italian dressing, barbecue sauce, garlic powder, onion powder, Accent, seasoned salt, and vinegar. Spread even amount on all sides of ribs. Cover and refrigerate 4 days. Preheat oven to 400 degrees. Pour Mountain Dew over ribs and cover with foil. Bake 1 hour at 400 degrees, then reduce heat to 350 degrees and bake 1½ to 2 hours. Over hot grill, cook ribs 8 minutes on each side. Brush with barbecue sauce while grilling. Taste compares to steakhouse ribs.

MRS. JONI LILLIE HOSTETLER, Edinboro, PA

Bar-B-Que Ribs

Racks of ribs
½ cup soy sauce
½ cup Worcestershire sauce
½ cup oil
1 teaspoon ginger
1 teaspoon dry mustard
3 to 6 whole cloves, ground
1 teaspoon Accent
Barbecue sauce

Put ribs in roaster. In bowl, mix soy sauce, Worcestershire sauce, oil, ginger, dry mustard, cloves, and Accent. Pour over ribs and fill roaster with water until ribs are covered. Bake 3 hours at 275 degrees. Place ribs on hot grill, basting with barbecue sauce, for at least 10 minutes, turning at least once.

MRS. LEVI MAST, Apple Creek, OH

Flavorful Flank Steak

½ cup soy sauce
½ cup vegetable oil
3 tablespoons barbecue sauce
3 tablespoons Worcestershire sauce
2 tablespoons dried minced onion
1 tablespoon liquid smoke (optional)
½ teaspoon garlic powder
1½ pounds beef flank steak

In large resealable plastic bag, combine soy sauce, vegetable oil, barbecue sauce, Worcestershire sauce, minced onion, liquid smoke, and garlic powder. Add steak, seal bag, and turn to coat. Refrigerate 8 hours or overnight. Drain and discard marinade. Grill steak, covered, over medium-high heat 6 to 8 minutes on each side or until meat reaches desired doneness. Meat thermometer should read 140 degrees for rare; 160 degrees for medium; or 170 degrees for well done. Slice steak across grain.

MENNO AND ESTHER YODER, Berlin, PA

Barbecue Steak

6 pounds ½ inch-thick T-bone or rib eye steak	Barbecue sauce (optional)
¾ cup salt	Accent
Lukewarm water	Garlic powder
	Onion powder

Put steak in bowl, add salt and lukewarm water. Let sit 3 hours. Preheat grill to 350 to 450 degrees. Coat each side of steak with barbecue sauce, if desired, and sprinkle with Accent, garlic powder, and onion powder. Grill steak 4 minutes on each side until there is only a thin layer of pink in center.

Mrs. Joni Lillie Hostetler, Edinboro, PA

Marinated Steak

½ cup soy sauce	1 teaspoon seasoned salt
½ cup Worcestershire sauce	½ teaspoon garlic powder
¼ cup olive oil	2 pounds steak or chicken breast

Mix soy sauce, Worcestershire sauce, olive oil, seasoned salt, and garlic powder. Pour over steak. Marinate 24 hours in refrigerator, then at room temperature 4 to 6 hours. Grill 7 minutes on each side at 500 degrees.

Mrs. Edna Yoder, Mifflintown, PA

Cream Cheese–Stuffed Backstrap

Backstrap of venison	Cream cheese
Marinade	Bacon

Marinate backstrap 4 hours or up to 2 days in your favorite seasoning. Preheat grill to 400 degrees (direct heat). Cut backstrap in half lengthwise. Don't cut all the way through, leaving about ½ inch. Lay backstrap open like you would a hot dog bun. Spread cream cheese on 1 side and press sides of backstrap back together. Wrap strips of bacon around backstrap. Grill approximately 30 minutes or until bacon is crisp.

Betty Sue Miller, Millersburg, OH

GRILLING LOINS AND ROASTS

- Brine loins or roasts for 3 to 5 days. Drain and season well with barbecue seasoning. Wrap meat with bacon, using toothpicks to hold in place. Grill to desired doneness.

JACOB JR. AND SADIE KING, Greenfork, IN

- Never cook a roast cold. Let it sit for at least 1 hour at room temperature. Brush with oil before and during roasting. The oil will seal in the juices.

LIZZIE ANN SWARTZENTRUBER, Newcomerstown, OH

BARBECUED BRISKET

1 (10 ounce) bottle
  soy sauce
2 tablespoons liquid
  smoke (optional)
1 tablespoon
  Worcestershire sauce
2 teaspoons pepper

1 teaspoon seasoned salt
1 teaspoon onion salt
1 teaspoon celery salt
1 teaspoon garlic salt
1 (5 pound) fresh
  beef brisket

In large resealable plastic bag, combine soy sauce, liquid smoke, Worcestershire sauce, pepper, seasoned salt, onion salt, celery salt, and garlic salt. Add brisket, seal bag, and turn to coat steak. Refrigerate 8 hours or overnight. Drain and discard marinade. Grill until done. Remove brisket from heat and let stand several minutes. Thinly slice across grain. Place in ungreased cake pan. Pour sauce* over meat. Cover and bake 1 hour or until heated through.

*SAUCE:

1 (14 ounce) bottle ketchup
1 to 2 tablespoons sugar
1 tablespoon vinegar
1½ teaspoons mustard

1½ teaspoons
  Worcestershire sauce
1 teaspoon soy sauce
Barbecue sauce to taste

Combine all ingredients and stir well.

MENNO AND ESTHER YODER, Berlin, PA

Smoked Brisket

1½ cups oil
¾ cup soy sauce
½ cup Worcestershire
   sauce
¼ cup vinegar
⅓ cup lemon juice
2 teaspoons dry mustard

1 teaspoon pepper
2 teaspoons parsley
2 cloves garlic, minced
5 pounds brisket
Barbecue sauce
Salt

Mix oil, soy sauce, Worcestershire sauce, vinegar, lemon juice, mustard, pepper, parsley, and garlic thoroughly. Pour over brisket and marinate 4 to 6 days in refrigerator. When ready to smoke, sprinkle brisket with barbecue sauce and salt. Smoke 10 hours at 250 degrees. Feeds 10 to 15 people.

Sam Glick, Bird-in-Hand, PA

GRILLED LEMON PEPPER SHRIMP

8 tablespoons lemon juice
¼ cup butter, melted
3 tablespoons
   Worcestershire sauce

15 extra-large shrimp
Salt
Lemon pepper seasoning

Combine lemon juice, butter, and Worcestershire sauce. Add shrimp, and gently coat with marinade. Refrigerate 1 hour. Grill at 300 to 400 degrees for approximately 10 minutes, turning once. Sprinkle with salt and lemon pepper seasoning to taste.

NATHAN AND LAURA HOCHSTETLER, Loudonville, OH

SOUTHERN BBQ SHRIMP

1 cup unsalted
   butter, melted
½ cup Worcestershire
   sauce
½ cup fresh lemon juice
1 tablespoon lemon zest
3 tablespoons golden
   brown sugar, packed

6 tablespoons Old
   Bay seasoning
2 pounds raw jumbo
   shrimp, thawed
Lemon wedges
Crispy baguette slices

Preheat grill to medium high. In large mixing bowl, combine butter, Worcestershire sauce, lemon juice, lemon zest, brown sugar, and seasoning. Stir well and divide into 2 equal portions. Thread shrimp onto 20 skewers and place in large, flat baking dish or gallon resealable plastic bag. Pour 1 portion of marinade over shrimp and cover. Refrigerate for at least 35 minutes (or 4 to 6 hours for better flavor). Place skewers on hot grill and cook 2 to 3 minutes on each side. Arrange shrimp on serving platter and drizzle with second portion of marinade. Garnish with lemon wedges and serve with crispy baguette slices.

BARBARA DETWEILER, Quaker City, OH

Grilling Fish and Seafood

Steaks and fillets − ½ inch − over hot grill − 2 to 3 minutes per side

Steaks and fillets −1 inch − over hot grill − 6 to 10 minutes per side

Whole fish or large fillets − 1 to 7 pounds − over low coals − about 10 minutes per inch of thickness or until meat thermometer reads 120 degrees.

Shrimp − medium (30 to 36 per pound) − over hot grill − 2 to 3 minutes per side

Sarah Ann Miller, Nashville, MI

Recommended Internal Temperature for Meats

Ground beef, pork, and lamb . . . . 160°

Beef and lamb − roasts and steaks
Medium-rare . . . . 135°
Medium . . . . 140°
Medium-well . . . . 145°

Pork chops and roasts . . . . 145°

Whole chicken and turkey *(measured in the thigh)* . . . . 165–180°

Chicken legs and thighs. . . . . 165–180°

Chicken breast. . . . . 165°

Ground chicken and turkey. . . . . 165°

CAMPFIRE CHICKEN AND PEPPERS

Sweet bell peppers
Skinless, boneless chicken grilled
Bacon

Cut peppers in half and remove seeds. Stuff peppers with grilled chicken that has been cut into strips. Wrap pepper with strips of bacon. Grill until bacon is crisp. Peppers can also be stuffed with hamburger, sausage, or cream cheese instead of chicken.

ESTHER MAST, Mercer, PA

Grilled Peppers

12 large jalapeños,
small bell peppers,
or Hungarian wax
semi-hot peppers

1 (8 ounce) package
cream cheese
1 pound bacon

Cut peppers in half lengthwise and remove seeds. Cut into quarters if large. Fill with cream cheese. Wrap with bacon slice secured with toothpicks. Place on hot grill until bacon is done.

Emma Byler, New Wilmington, PA
Ruth Byler, Quaker City, OH
Mrs. Chester (Rose) Miller, Centerville, PA
Barbara Shetler, Monroe, IN
Mrs. Rachel Yoder, Homer, MI

We do these on a campfire grate.
Fannie Ann Byler, Reynoldsville, PA

I season my cream cheese with ½ teaspoon garlic salt and ¼ teaspoon onion powder.
Mrs. Miller, Fredericksburg, OH

We cut off the stems, remove the seeds, and stuff cream cheese into the whole pepper.
Elizabeth K. Swarey, Charlotte Courthouse, VA

Buffalo Chicken Banana Peppers

1½ cups chopped
cooked chicken
8 ounces cream cheese
1 cup shredded cheese

1 tablespoon hot sauce
½ teaspoon salt
12 hot banana peppers,
halved and seeded

In medium bowl, stir together chicken, cream cheese, shredded cheese, hot sauce, and salt. Spoon mixture into pepper halves and place on hot grill, cooking until pepper is tender and browned. May also bake in oven 15 minutes at 400 degrees.

Emma Byler, New Wilmington, PA

GRILLED PEPPER POPPERS

10 to 12 hot or sweet
  banana peppers
8 ounces cream
  cheese, softened

1 cup shredded cheddar
6 ounces sausage, fried,
  drained, and crumbled
Bacon

Cut peppers in half lengthwise and remove seeds. In bowl, mix cream cheese, cheddar, and sausage. Fill peppers with mixture. Wrap bacon slice around each pepper half. Place on hot grill until bacon is done.

This has been one of my favorites since I was a little girl.
MALINDA M. GINGERICH, Spartansburg, PA

We use jalapeño peppers.
ALBERT AND AMANDA BYLER, Clarks Mills, PA

I do the same without the sausage.
ORPHA KEIM, Ashland, OH

We have also used small sweet peppers we call "fooled you" peppers.
MRS. DAVID LAMBRIGHT, Mount Vernon, OH
MRS. EDNA YODER, Mifflintown, PA

JALAPEÑO POPPERS

Jalapeño peppers
8 ounces cream
  cheese, softened

16 ounces sour cream
Bacon strips

Cut off tops of peppers and clean out seeds. In bowl, mix cream cheese and sour cream. Fill peppers with mixture. Wrap bacon strip around each pepper and secure with toothpick. Grill until bacon is done. Very good!

LIZZIE ANN L. KURTZ, New Wilmington, PA
KRISTINA MILLER, Monroe, IN

GRILLED CHEESE

Place string cheese in grill basket over low coals and grill until cheese is soft. You can sprinkle with seasonings like taco, ranch, or Greek.

L. BONTRAGER, Nappanee, IN

Stuffed Mushrooms

1 pound or 20 to 25 whole
  bite-sized mushrooms
4 ounces cream cheese
¼ to ½ cup shredded
  cheddar

1 tablespoon chopped
  onion (optional)
¼ teaspoon garlic powder
½ teaspoon onion salt
¼ teaspoon pepper
½ pound bacon

Separate stems from mushroom caps. In food processor, process
mushroom stems, cream cheese, cheddar, onion, garlic powder, onion
salt, and pepper until well mixed. Stuff mixture into mushroom caps.
Wrap strip of bacon around each cap and secure with toothpick. Grill
at 350 degrees 15 minutes on each side until bacon is done.

Sarah Byler, Knox, PA
Elizabeth Stoltzfus, Quarryville, PA

BACON-WRAPPED MUSHROOMS

1 box mushrooms
1 pound bacon

Wash mushrooms and wrap with bacon slice. Cook on grill or over campfire.

Mrs. Miller, Fredericksburg, OH

SIMPLE GRILLED STUFFED MUSHROOMS

Mushrooms
1 (8 ounce) package
cream cheese

¾ cup bacon bits
1 cup shredded cheddar

Clean mushrooms and remove stems. In bowl, mix cream cheese, bacon bits, and cheddar. Fill mushrooms with mixture. Place on grill 10 to 15 minutes.

Martha Beachy, Bulter, OH

Pizza Appetizers

Ritz crackers
Pizza sauce

Pepperoni
Shredded mozzarella

In grill basket, arrange layer of crackers. On each cracker put dab of pizza sauce, pepperoni slice, and spoonful of cheese. Place basket on grill over low heat. Cook until cheese is fully melted.

L. Bontrager, Nappanee, IN

Fruit Pizza

1 tube crescent rolls
Cream cheese
　pastry filling

Pie filling

Spread crescent rolls on greased air-bake pizza pan or pizza stone (when using stone, preheat first and dust with cornmeal). Grill at 350 degrees, indirect heat, 10 minutes or until golden brown. Put cream cheese on crust and top with pie filling. Eat warm.

Betty Sue Miller, Millersburg, OH

S'mores Chocolate Chip Cake

½ cup butter, softened
½ cup brown sugar
1 teaspoon vanilla
1 egg
1 cup flour
1 cup graham
　cracker crumbs

½ teaspoon baking
　powder
¼ teaspoon salt
½ cup chocolate chips
2 cups mini
　marshmallows

In bowl, cream butter and brown sugar. Add vanilla and egg and stir till fluffy. Add flour, graham cracker crumbs, baking powder, and salt. Press dough in 9-inch round metal pie pan, reserving ½ cup for topping. Sprinkle with chocolate chips and marshmallows. Top with crumbles of remaining dough. Bake at 350 degrees, indirect heat, 25 minutes or until top is lightly browned.

Betty Sue Miller, Millersburg, OH

Hot Chocolate

¼ cup brown sugar
2 tablespoons cocoa
⅛ teaspoon salt
¼ cup hot water

1 tablespoon butter
4 cups milk
1 teaspoon vanilla
12 large marshmallows

In saucepan on grill grate or grill's side burner, combine brown sugar, cocoa, and salt. Stir in hot water and butter. Bring to a boil. Add milk, vanilla, and marshmallows. Heat until hot, remove from heat, and let marshmallows melt for about 10 minutes. Stir and serve. Makes 5 servings.

Mrs. Roman (Alma) Yoder, Patriot, OH

Chai Tea Latte

6 cups water
3 chai tea bags

4 cups milk
1 cup maple syrup

In saucepan on grill grate or grill's side burner, boil water and steep tea 5 to 10 minutes. Remove tea bags. Add milk and maple syrup. Reheat but don't boil. Enjoy.

Anna Byler, Spartansburg, PA

RECIPES FOR NO COOKING ASSEMBLY

Life is 10 percent what you make it and 90 percent how you take it.

ANNA A. SLABAUGH, APPLE CREEK, OH

If you are camping without a kitchen or if you just want to be outside among friends, family, and their activities, this section contains some things you can mix up without cooking.

CAMPING COOLER TIPS

- Start with a chilled cooler. Place it in the refrigerator or fill it with cold water and/or ice several hours before packing it.

- Tape a small thermometer inside the top of the cooler to keep track of the temperature. It should register 40 degrees or less for safe food.

- Chill all food and drinks before packing them in the cooler. When possible, freeze food like meat beforehand so that it will stay cold even longer.

- Remove things from cardboard boxes or other permeable packaging to plastic storage bags and label clearly.

- Place things that need to stay coldest (e.g., meat and dairy) on the bottom of the cooler. Also, things that won't be needed until later in your trip should be on the bottom. Pack ice around those before adding a top layer of food and more ice. If you know you'll need something immediately, put that on top.

- Before leaving home, freeze bottles of water. They'll keep things cool, and when melted, you can use the water for drinking and cooking.

- Pack a separate cooler for things in highest demand, such as beverages. The more a cooler is opened, the more the temperature will fluctuate.

- Open the cooler only when necessary and reclose as quickly as possible.

- Keeping the cooler as full as possible will help to maintain the temperature.

- Set the cooler in the shade. Cover with a blanket for extra insulation.

Recipes for No Cooking Assembly

Overnight Oatmeal

1 cup old-fashioned rolled oats	2¼ teaspoons cinnamon
1 cup milk	2 to 3 tablespoons flaxseed
1 cup Greek yogurt (plain or flavored)	¾ cup chopped fresh fruit

Stir together oats, milk, yogurt, cinnamon, flaxseed, and fruit. Spoon into half-pint canning jars. Place lids on tightly and chill overnight. In the morning, open jars and add extra fruit if you wish. These will stay fresh for several days if kept chilled. Excellent for an easy campsite breakfast.

Emma Byler, New Wilmington, PA

Coffee Bites

2 cups quick oats
1½ cups peanut butter
¾ cup dark
  chocolate chips
½ cup honey
¼ cup coffee grounds
¼ cup chia seeds

Mix all ingredients together and form into balls. Store in cool place or refrigerate. This is a perfect snack for a camping trip.

Janet Weaver, Lititz, PA

Fiber Balls

3 cups oatmeal
1 cup crisp rice cereal
1 cup chocolate chips
1 cup raisins
1 cup peanut butter
½ cup shredded
  coconut (optional)
½ cup ground flaxseed

Mix all ingredients together and form into balls. Refrigerate. This is a nice snack to pack for sitting around a campfire.

Martha Mast, North Bloomfield, OH

Protein Bars

3 cups oatmeal
1 cup shredded coconut
1 cup peanut butter
½ cup flaxseed
¼ cup chia seeds
⅛ cup water
½ cup coconut oil
½ cup white grape juice
2 scoops protein powder
1 cup chocolate chips

In large bowl, mix all ingredients and press into 9x13-inch pan. Cut into squares or rectangles. Easy to pack and take camping.

Katieann J. Gingerich, Howard, OH

COATED GRAPES

1 cup sour cream
½ cup powdered sugar
8 ounces cream
  cheese, softened

1 teaspoon vanilla
Grapes

Mix sour cream, powdered sugar, cream cheese, and vanilla. Add grapes and stir to coat. Chill.

MARLENE JOY STOLTZFUS, Gap, PA
ESTHER J. GINGERICH, Fredericksburg, OH

CREAMY QUICK FRUIT SALAD

1 (8 ounce) carton
  whipped topping
1 (16 ounce) carton
  cottage cheese
⅓ cup orange gelatin mix

1 (10 ounce) can crushed
  pineapple, drained
1 (11 ounce) can mandarin
  oranges, drained

In bowl, fold together whipped topping, cottage cheese, and gelatin mix. Stir in pineapple and mandarin oranges. Refrigerate for several hours before serving. This is a great salad or dessert for serving at a hot dog roast.

ESTHER D. SCHWARTZ, Harrisville, PA

Corn Chip Salad

1 to 2 heads lettuce, chopped
1 pound bacon, fried and chopped
6 hard-boiled eggs, chopped
1½ cups shredded cheese
4 to 6 cups crushed corn chips

In large bowl, layer lettuce, bacon, eggs, and cheese. Just before serving, add chips, and toss with dressing below.

Dressing:

¼ cup sugar
¼ cup brown sugar
¼ cup milk
1 cup salad dressing (like Miracle Whip)
1 to 2 tablespoons vinegar

Mix all ingredients together until well combined and pour over salad.

Susan Byler, Mercer, PA
Elizabeth J. Miller, Navarre, OH

Simple Tomato Salad

1 quart diced tomatoes
2 tablespoons diced onion
¼ cup diced green pepper
¼ cup sugar
2 tablespoons vinegar
1 teaspoon salt

Mix all ingredients together. Very good!

Emma Miller, Ashland, OH

Grilled Chicken Salad

Great for using leftover meat.

2 cups grilled chicken,
  chopped and chilled
¾ cup finely diced celery
4 hard-boiled eggs,
  chopped or sliced

1 cup mayonnaise
Onion, diced
Dill pickles, diced

Mix chicken, celery, eggs, and mayonnaise. Add onion and pickles to suit your taste. Can be served in hollowed-out tomato on bed of romaine lettuce.

Mary A. Horning, East Earl, PA

BLT Chicken Salad

1 head lettuce, chopped
1 pound boneless,
  skinless chicken breast,
  grilled and chopped

1 pound bacon, fried
  and crumbled
1 package shredded
  cheese
1 pint cherry tomatoes

Layer ingredients in large bowl or casserole dish starting with lettuce, then chicken, bacon, cheese, and tomatoes.

Dressing:

1/2 cup salad dressing
  or mayonnaise
3 to 4 tablespooms
  barbecue sauce

1 tablespoon apple
  cider vinegar
1 to 2 tablespoons sugar

In mixing bowl, blend salad dressing, barbecue sauce, vinegar, and sugar. Pour over salad and mix. Our favorite salad!

Jessie and Rosanna Bontrager, Constable, NY

Salad on a Bun

Ranch dressing:

4 ounces cream cheese
½ cup ranch dressing
½ cup sour cream

¼ cup sugar
½ teaspoon salt

Mix all ingredients together.

Salad:

12 hamburger buns
Lettuce
Broccoli
Cucumbers, sliced

Tomatoes, sliced
Shredded cheese
Bacon bits

Spread dressing on buns then layer with toppings starting with lettuce, then broccoli, cucumbers, tomatoes, cheese, and bacon bits. Top with bun spread with dressing.

Esther Mast, Mercer, PA

Fresh Garden Salsa

4 cups diced tomatoes, drained well in colander	½ cup chopped fresh parsley
½ cup very finely diced onion	¼ cup chopped fresh cilantro
1 large green bell pepper, diced	1 tablespoon vinegar
2 cups diced cucumber	1 tablespoon lemon juice
	½ teaspoon cumin
	Dash pepper

Mix all ingredients together and refrigerate 4 hours before serving. Very refreshing and goes well served with corn chips or tacos.

Variation: Add 2 cups fresh-cut corn and 1 can black beans, drained and rinsed.

KATHRYN TROYER, Rutherford, TN

Quick Veggie Dip

1 cup ranch dressing
1 cup salad dressing, mayonnaise, sour cream, or plain yogurt

For a quick and easy veggie dip, mix equal parts ranch dressing with salad dressing. Mix well.

EMMA MILLER, Ashland, OH

Pepperoni Pizza Dip

1 (8 ounce) package cream cheese, softened	Salsa
8 ounces sour cream	Pepperoni
	Mozzarella

Mix cream cheese, sour cream, and salsa. Layer in dish with pepperoni and mozzarella. Serve with your favorite chips. This is a great "take along" for evenings by the campfire.

PRISCILLA SCHMUCKER, Millerton, PA

CARAMEL DIP

8 ounces cream cheese
¾ cup brown sugar
1 cup sour cream
2 teaspoons vanilla
2 teaspoons lemon juice

1 (3 ounce) package
instant vanilla
pudding mix
1 cup milk

Beat cream cheese and brown sugar until smooth. Add sour cream, vanilla, and lemon juice. Beat. Add pudding mix and milk. Again, beat well. Serve with fresh fruit.

LAURA MILLER, Mount Vernon, OH

FRUIT DIP

1 (12 ounce) jar marshmallow crème
8 ounces cream cheese, softened
1 tablespoon orange juice

Mix all ingredients well and chill. Serve with apples, oranges, and the like.

LYDIA A. GLICK, Port Washington, OH

YOGURT FRUIT DESSERT

1 (16 ounce) carton
  whipped topping
1 quart vanilla yogurt
1 cup instant vanilla
  pudding mix

2 cans mandarin
  oranges, drained
1 can crushed or
  chunk pineapple
Grapes

In large bowl, mix whipped topping, yogurt, and pudding mix. Add oranges. Drain off some of the pineapple juice and add pineapple and grapes as desired. A very light and refreshing summertime dessert.

MRS. JACOB (LEANNA) YODER, Patriot, OH

No-Bake Party Mix

Potato sticks
Goldfish crackers
Cheese crackers
Cheetos Crunchy
  Cheese snacks
Cheerios
Chex cereal, corn or rice
Bugles corn snacks
Pretzel sticks

Peanuts
6 ounces olive oil
4 tablespoons ranch
  powder seasoning
2 tablespoons cheddar
  cheese powder
2 tablespoons sour cream
  and onion powder

In 13-quart bowl, place your choice mix of potato sticks, goldfish crackers, cheese crackers, Cheetos, Cheerios, Chex cereal, Bugles, pretzels, peanuts, and whatever else you desire until almost full. In bowl, mix olive oil with ranch, cheese, and sour cream and onion powders. Place dry mixture in 1 or more bags. Add seasoning mixture and shake to coat well. Shake bag(s) every 15 minutes for 2 hours. Serve.

RUBEN AND RUTH SCHWARTZ, Willshire, OH

Replenishment Drink

1 teaspoon ginger	½ cup sugar
2 tablespoons vinegar	1 quart water

Mix and serve over ice. Refreshing for when you have been working out in the heat.

EMMA BYLER, New Wilmington. PA

Fresh-Squeezed Lemonade

5 to 6 lemons	Water
2 cups sugar	Ice

Slice 1 lemon for garnish. Squeeze juice from remaining lemons. Add sugar and enough water and ice to make 1 full gallon.

MARLENE JOY STOLTZFUS, Gap, PA

Iced Coffee

4 teaspoons instant coffee	½ teaspoon salt
1 tablespoon cold water	2 quarts ice-cold milk
1 cup brown sugar	

Dissolve instant coffee in water. In pitcher, combine brown sugar, salt, and milk. Add coffee, mixing well until all is dissolved. Very refreshing on a warm summer day.

MIRIAM COBLENTZ, Greenfield, OH

Root Beer

2 cups sugar
2 cups hot water
4 teaspoons root
  beer extract

Lukewarm water
1 teaspoon yeast

Melt sugar with hot water and pour into gallon jug. Add extract. Fill jug with lukewarm water. Add yeast. Set jug in sun for 3 hours, then put in cold place until next day. Great to serve on a hot summer day.

ANNA A. SLABAUGH, **Apple Creek, OH**

Sun Tea

4 tea bags
1 gallon water

Place tea bags and water in gallon glass jug (I prefer a clear jug). Set jug in sun until water is fully colored. Take out tea bags and sweeten to preferred taste. Add lemon juice if desired.

BETTY BYLER, **Brockway, PA**

Mennonite Wine

12 ounces grape juice
16 ounces orange juice
¼ cup lemon juice
1½ cups water

1 cup sugar
2 liters ginger ale or
  lemon-lime soda
Ice

In gallon pitcher, mix grape juice and orange juice. Add lemon juice, water, and sugar, stirring until sugar dissolves. Add ginger ale. Add ice to make 1 gallon.

SUSAN BYLER, **Mercer, PA**

Orange Drink for a Crowd

    3 jars orange drink mix
    10 gallons cold water
    1 (2 liter) bottle orange soda

In 10-gallon milk can, dissolve drink mix in water. Before serving, add orange soda. Yields approximately 100 servings.

Fannie L. Stuzman, West Salem, OH

Sparkling Drink

    2 (12 ounce) cans orange, pineapple, or apple concentrate
    4 cans cold water
    2½ cans ginger ale or lemon-lime soda

Combine all ingredients in gallon jug and stir well. Makes 1 gallon of very refreshing drink.

Keri Barkman, Napp, IN

Vanilla Ice Cream

12 egg yolks
1½ cups maple syrup
3 tablespoons vanilla
1 teaspoon maple
    flavoring

3 tablespoons arrowroot
10 cups heavy cream
12 egg whites, beaten

In mixing bowl, beat egg yolks and blend in maple syrup, vanilla, maple flavoring, arrowroot, and heavy cream. Fold in beaten egg whites. Pour into 6-quart ice cream freezer and freeze according to ice cream maker's instructions.

MARTY AND LAURA MILLER, Hillsboro, OH

Snowcream

1 cup milk
½ teaspoon vanilla

½ cup sugar
Snow

Mix milk, vanilla, and sugar. Stir in snow a little at a time until it is as thick as ice cream. Fun for children on a snowy day.

JACOB JR. AND SADIE KING, Greenfork, IN

Recipes for Marinades and Sauces

Half of our lives is spent trying to find something to do with the time we have rushed through life trying to save.

AMISH PROVERB

Meat simply salted can be quite good when cooked outdoors, but sometimes you want a little more to bring out the flavor or to help with a tougher cut of meat. Try these sauces and marinades.

Recipes for Marinades and Sauces

Hot Dog Sauce

½ green pepper, minced
1 medium onion, minced
¾ cup ketchup
2 tablespoons
  brown sugar
2 tablespoons mustard
1 tablespoon
  Worcestershire sauce
¾ teaspoon salt

Mix all ingredients together, blending well.

Barbara Coblentz, Greenfield, OH

Big Mac Sauce

1 cup Miracle Whip
  salad dressing
⅓ cup pickle relish
¼ cup french dressing
1 tablespoon
  minced onion
1 tablespoon sugar
¼ teaspoon pepper

Mix all ingredients together, blending well.

Katie M. Beiler, Parkesburg, PA
Lizzie Ann L. Kurtz, New Wilmington, PA

Chick-fil-A Sauce

½ cup mayonnaise
2 tablespoons honey
1 tablespoon smoky
  barbecue sauce
2 teaspoons mustard
½ teaspoon lemon juice
½ teaspoon liquid smoke

Whisk all ingredients together until well blended. Enjoy with chicken, potatoes, or other. Tastes very similar to the real Chick-fil-A sauce.

Glenda Schwartz, Milford, IN

Garlic Spread

1 cup butter, softened
4 tablespoons
mayonnaise
6 cloves garlic, minced
4 teaspoons oregano
2 teaspoons salt
2 teaspoons pepper
½ teaspoon sage
(optional)

Mix all ingredients together, blending well. Spread on bread slice and toast or serve on sandwiches. Just a thin layer gives a lot of flavor!

Mary King, Kinzers, PA

Honey Mustard Sauce

½ cup mayonnaise
1 tablespoon Dijon
mustard
1 tablespoon yellow
mustard
3 tablespoons honey
1 teaspoon apple
cider vinegar
⅛ teaspoon garlic powder
⅛ teaspoon paprika
⅛ teaspoon salt
Sprinkle pepper

Combine all ingredients and stir until smooth. Chill. Great dipping sauce for pigs in a blanket or whatever you like.

Mrs. Levi Mast, Apple Creek, OH

Fresh Horseradish Sauce

1 pound horseradish root
1 cup vinegar
1 teaspoon salt
½ teaspoon sugar

Put all ingredients in blender and blend until well processed and mixed. Store in refrigerator. Lasts for months.

Anna Byler, Spartansburg, PA

Western Burger Barbecue Sauce

1 cup ketchup
½ cup vinegar
½ cup water

3 tablespoons
brown sugar
1 tablespoon
Worcestershire sauce
or liquid smoke

Combine all ingredients in saucepan and boil 10 minutes. Pour over grilled hamburgers and serve while hot.

Janet Weaver, Lititz, PA

Simple Bar-B-Q Sauce

2 cups ketchup
1 cup brown sugar
2 tablespoons mustard

Mix all ingredients together, blending well. Very good on ribs, pork chops, and burgers.

Ida Byler, Spartansburg, PA

Sweet-Bold BBQ Sauce (to can)

32 cups ketchup
9 cups Sucanat or
   brown sugar
6 cups molasses
2½ cups pineapple juice
1½ cups Worcestershire
   sauce
1 cup natural smoke
   flavoring
1 cup apple cider vinegar

1 cup ground mustard
1 cup sea salt
½ cup smoked paprika
⅓ cup garlic powder
½ cup pepper
1 teaspoon stevia powder
   (adjust to taste)
½ teaspoon cayenne
   (optional)

Mix all ingredients together in large kettle. Bring to slow boil for 1 hour to let sugars caramelize and flavors meld. Stir occasionally. Put into canning jars with lids and heat in water bath 10 minutes to seal. Makes approximately 12 quarts.

Very delicious and goes well with grilled meats.
Jacob Jr. and Sadie King, Greenfork, IN

Steakhouse Butter

½ cup butter, softened
2 tablespoons finely
minced red onion
1 clove garlic,
finely minced
1 tablespoon parsley

½ tablespoon thyme
2 tablespoons of your
favorite vinegar
Sprinkle salt
Dash pepper

Stir all ingredients together until thoroughly combined. Scoop butter into ziplock bag. Form butter into thick log roughly 4 inches long. Tightly roll up bag. Refrigerate or freeze for several hours or overnight until butter is firm enough to slice. Top each steak or pork chop with thick slice of steakhouse butter shortly before removing steaks from grill.

BETTY SUE MILLER, Millersburg, OH

Steak and Burger Seasoning

2½ tablespoons salt
1 tablespoon pepper

1½ to 3 tablespoons
brown sugar
1 tablespoon smoked
paprika

Mix all ingredients together, adjusting amount of brown sugar to your taste. Put in shaker container. Use to generously season both sides of steaks and burgers. For best results, season meat the day before grilling.

Mary A. Horning, East Earl, PA

Taco Seasoning

9 teaspoons chili powder
9 teaspoons paprika
13½ teaspoons cumin
18 teaspoons
parsley flakes

9 teaspoons onion powder
4½ teaspoons garlic salt
4½ teaspoons oregano

Mix and store in airtight container. Seven teaspoons mix equal 1 store-bought package.

Linda Burkholder, Fresno, OH

Barbecue Chicken Spray

3 pounds butter
5 ounces lemon juice
4½ ounces Worcestershire sauce

In saucepan, combine butter, lemon juice, and Worcestershire sauce. Bring to a boil and remove from heat. Cool slightly and put into spray bottle.

To use: Salt chicken the day before you plan to grill. Spray mixture on chicken often while grilling to 185 degrees internal temperature. Spray can also be used on potatoes before grilling.

Rachel Miller, Millersburg, OH

Marinade and Spray for Chicken

Marinade:

10 cups cold water
1 cup Morton Tender Quick
4 tablespoons liquid smoke

Mix all ingredients together. Pour over chicken and refrigerate 2 hours. Spray grilling chicken often with mixture below.

Spray:

½ gallon vinegar
1 quart water
½ pound browned butter
1 (5 ounce) bottle Worcestershire sauce
⅓ cup salt

In saucepan, combine all ingredients and heat to boiling. Remove from heat. Pour into spray bottle. Shake before each spray.

Martha Beachy, Bulter, OH

Simple Barbecued Chicken Brine

1 cup vinegar
¼ cup salt
1 ounce Worcestershire sauce

In saucepan, heat all ingredients. Cool and pour over chicken. Soak 3 days before grilling.

Clara Miller, Walhonding, OH

Worth-Waiting-For Chicken Marinade

2 cups vinegar
2 cups water
1 cup butter or olive oil
⅓ cup salt

5 tablespoons Worcestershire sauce
½ teaspoon pepper
2 tablespoons barbecue seasoning

In saucepan, mix vinegar, water, butter, salt, Worcestershire sauce, pepper, and barbecue seasoning. Heat to boiling. Pour over chicken and marinate 24 hours in refrigerator. Grill chicken over medium-hot coals.

Amanda Byler, Curwensville, PA

Brine for Grilling Meat

3 quarts water
¼ cup Morton
  Tender Quick
¼ cup brown sugar

1 tablespoon
  Worcestershire sauce
¼ cup salt

Mix all ingredients together. Pour over meat and marinate 2 days. Can be used on any meat. Makes very juicy and tender pork chops.

Mrs. Levi Mast, Apple Creek, OH

Marinated Pork

¾ cup vegetable oil
⅓ cup soy sauce
¼ cup vinegar
2 tablespoons
  Worcestershire sauce
1 tablespoon lemon juice

1 tablespoon mustard
1 clove garlic, minced
1 teaspoon salt
1 teaspoon pepper
1 tablespoon dried
  parsley flakes

Mix all ingredients together. Pour over cubes of pork or chicken. Refrigerate 4 to 6 hours. Place meat in grill basket or on heavy-duty aluminum foil. Grill, basting occasionally with marinade.

Mrs. Reuben N. Byler, Dayton, PA

Asian Steak Marinade

1 cup soy sauce
½ cup vinegar
1½ teaspoons pepper
¾ cup brown sugar
2 cloves garlic, minced
½ cup water
½ cup oil

Mix all ingredients together and marinate steak in mixture for several hours. Grill as desired.

Emma Byler, New Wilmington, PA

Steak Sauce Marinade

½ cup sweet-spicy steak sauce or barbecue sauce
¼ cup Worcestershire sauce
¼ cup onion flakes
2 tablespoons lemon juice
2 tablespoons oil
¾ teaspoon garlic powder

Mix all ingredients together and marinate steak in mixture for 2 hours before grilling.

Janet Weaver, Lititz, PA

Advice for Enjoying the Great Outdoors

*There is not one blade of grass, there
is no color in this world that is not
intended to make us rejoice.*

John Calvin

Each season is full of the wonders of God's hand upon creation. Whether it is the snow of winter, the buds of spring, the fruit of summer, or the colors of fall, there is something to be enjoyed outdoors all year round. May you take time to spend a little time outdoors each day, soaking up some vitamin D from the sun, breathing in the fresh air, listening to the songs of birds, and letting go of life's pressures.

BIRDIE BUGGY

I heard a wren calling.
I looked outside to see
A pair of pretty wren birds
In my little birdie buggy.
Chirping in the sunshine,
They sang their songs of cheer.
They seemed to say that springtime
Once again was here.
Those pretty cheery wren birds
Oh, how I love to see
Them sitting on their birdie buggy
In my silver maple tree.
God gives to us the wrens.
He gives us birds of spring,
Cheering us with songs
And with the songs they sing.
Singing in the sunlight,
Singing cheerfully,
Lifting up our spirits
With their melody.

RUTH BYLER, Quaker City, OH

ADVICE for ENJOYING the GREAT OUTDOORS

OUTDOOR FUN

EASY CAMPFIRE

- Whenever you have twigs in the yard, put them in your firepit. Place a small cardboard box or newspaper underneath, then keep piling on twigs as they fall from trees. Children love to put twigs in the firepit in anticipation of a campfire. When you are ready for a campfire, your starter is ready to light.

- Don't throw out the top dome lid of an old grill. Keep it to put on top of your firepit to keep stored twigs dry. It is also good for covering burgers or hot dogs when grilling on a fire grate. And it will keep rain off your fire in a sudden downpour.

BARBIE ESH, Paradise, PA

FIRE STARTERS

- Fill an egg carton loosely with wood shavings. Pour melted candle wax or paraffin over shavings. Let harden and break into pieces to use for fire starter.

MRS. LEVI MILLER, Junction City, OH

- Make fire starters out of old bath towels. Cut them into strips about 2 inches wide by 12 to 15 inches long. Starting at short end, roll up strips. Use kitchen tongs to dip each roll into old candle wax that has been melted. Then set rolls in cardboard egg carton. Cut cup sections of carton apart. Use a section or two to get fire started easily.

BARBIE ESH, Paradise, PA

Color-Changing Pine Cones

1 gallon hot water
1 teaspoon dish soap

1 pound (no more)
Epsom salt, rock
salt, or baking soda
Pine cones

In large plastic bucket, mix hot water, dish soap, and salt. Add pine cones and weigh them down to keep them submerged. Soak 24 hours. Remove pine cones and place on newspaper to dry thoroughly. Add pine cones to campfire when it has burned down almost to embers, and watch colors flicker as they burn.

SUSIE KING, **Allenwood, PA**

Yard Games

Hide-and-seek is the favorite game at our place.

Our family, my uncle's family, and my sister's family all gather at my grandparents' house most Sunday evenings. The children are aged fifteen and down. They will play hide-and-seek as usual but with a twist of their own.

Whenever someone gets "free," he or she has a bonus point. These points are tallied up over the evening until someone has ten. That person is the winner for the evening's game.

With this twist, the game is fun for all ages. The older ones have their own competition with the bonus points, but the younger ones can still help.

RACHEL STOLTZFUS, **Paradise, PA**

Bubbles

⅓ cup dish soap
1½ cups water

2 teaspoons sugar
1 drop food coloring

Combine all ingredients and pour into old bubble container or jar. Use bubble wand to blow bubbles.

As a small girl, I loved to make my own bubbles!
MARLENE JOY STOLTZFUS, **Gap, PA**

Giant Homemade Bubbles

1 dishpan
6 cups water
2 cups dish soap
  (Ivory or Joy)

¾ cup corn syrup
1 plastic coat hanger

Fill dishpan with room-temperature water. Add dish soap and corn syrup. Mix well. Dip coat hanger into mixture. Wave coat hanger gently to create giant bubbles.

Elsie Schlabach, Big Prairie, OH

Sharing with Wild Birds

- Take leftover church peanut butter or old peanut butter and smear it on a tree trunk. Watch the birds enjoy it.

  MALINDA M. GINGERICH, Spartansburg, PA

- Pour bacon grease over pieces of leftover toast or bread. Let harden, then run a string through the center and tie it to a tree branch for birds.

  MALINDA M. GINGERICH, Spartansburg, PA

Hummingbird Feed

1 cup sugar	Red food coloring
4 cups boiling water	(optional)

Dissolve sugar in boiling water. Add food coloring if desired. Let cool, then pour into hummingbird feeder and hang where you can watch your new friends come for a snack.

MARLENE JOY STOLTZFUS, Gap, PA

Bird Suet

1 cup crunchy peanut butter	2 cups quick oats
1 cup lard or bacon grease	2 cups cornmeal
	1 cup flour
	⅓ cup sugar

In saucepan, melt peanut butter and lard. Stir in remaining ingredients. Line 9x13-inch pan with waxed paper. Pour suet into pan. Cool. Cut into 6 squares. Hang in suet feeder and watch birds enjoy their treat. Keep extra suet squares in freezer until ready to use.

MARLENE JOY STOLTZFUS, Gap, PA

Outdoor Cooking Tips

Prepare Ahead

Before you head outdoors, plan your menu. Whenever possible, prepare ingredients at home before packing them up to go outside or to a campsite. Chop vegetables, slice meat, shred cheese, boil eggs, precook meat for stuffing peppers or quick soups, and so on. Store them in plastic ziplock bags that pack easily into coolers.

Keep It Cold

To keep food cold if you don't have ice packs, put a gallon-sized ziplock bag inside another bag of the same size. Fill inside bag with ice. Squeeze out air and seal both bags. Put inside carrier before adding your cold dish.

MARY K. BONTRAGER, Middlebury, IN

Keep It Hot

Put your hot meat in an ice chest lined with aluminum foil. It will stay hot for hours.

AMANDA ZEHR, Spencerville, IN

Spice Container

Reuse small containers like a Tic Tac holder to put spices in for camping.

Reuse Bottles

Reuse squeeze bottles or disposable water bottles for ketchup and salad dressing. They are also good to put pancake batter or beaten eggs in to take outside for cooking.

Keep It Covered

Always use lids to cover food while cooking. Not only does food cook faster, but lids keep bugs out.

Butter

When cooking outdoors, set butter dish in pan of cold salt water to keep butter hard.

Salomie E. Glick, **Howard, PA**

Ice Cream

Wrap wet newspaper around ice cream containers. It may freeze on in places. Cover with more dry newspaper. The ice cream should not melt during transport or while serving outdoors.

Anna M. Yoder, **Mercer, MO**

Stretching Ground Meat

Ground meat can be stretched by adding quick oats and moistening them with tomato juice for less expensive burgers.

Mrs. Bethany Martin, **Homer City, PA**

Meat Ready?

To tell when grilled meat is ready to turn over, wait until you see juice on top. Then it is ready to turn.

Sadie Byler, **Reynoldsville, PA**

Juicy Meat

A fork or knife should never be stuck into meat that is frying or grilling because it lets juices out. When done cooking, remove meat from heat using spatula or tongs and let rest before cutting into it so juices have time to settle into meat.

Hamburgers

When frying or grilling a hamburger, punch a small hole in the middle of it. It will get done quicker.

EMMA BYLER, New Wilmington. PA

Leftover Grilled Meat

Leftover grilled chicken, hamburgers, or hot dogs need not go to waste. Make use of them in your next meal by creating chicken sub sandwiches, chicken salad, or steak salad. Cut the meat and use inside a pie iron sandwich. Chop the meat and add to a pot of soup or beans. In fact, you might want to plan to cook more meat than needed just so you have a head start on your next meal.

Monitor Your Smoker

Use a baby monitor to keep an eye on the temperature on your smoker while you are doing other things.

Easy Cleanup

When you empty pots of food, always put some hot water in pot and tightly replace lid. Set aside. Your pots will be much easier to clean.

SUSIE KINSINGER, Fredericktown, OH

Washing Dishes

A good way to dry clean dishes while outdoors is to put them in a mesh bag and hang it from a tree.

Secure Your Food

Don't leave food, leftovers, or dirty dishes out where wildlife will be drawn to them. No one enjoys raccoons tearing through the backyard or campsite on the hunt for an easy meal.

Campsite Tips

Match Holder

Keep matches in small jelly jar. Cut a circle of sandpaper to place in lid for a striker.

Picnic Tables

- Mint repels flies. Spray peppermint oil mixed in water on and around picnic table before setting out food. Or put peppermint oil on a napkin or clean cloth placed on table.

Ellen Miller, Dowling, MI

- When eating outside, lay tea leaves on table between food dishes to keep flies away.
- When you are having a cookout or picnic and don't have tablecloth clips, bend wide-mouth canning jar lids in half so they are D-shaped, and slide them over cloth and edge of table.

Mary K. Bontrager, Middlebury, IN

Wet Shoes

If your shoes or hiking boots get wet while camping, stuff them with newspaper, paper towel, a dry shirt, or towel. Moisture should be mostly absorbed overnight. Works even better if placed near the campfire for the addition of heat.

Sticking Zipper

A little candle wax or lip balm rubbed on a zipper of a jacket, tent, or duffel bag can help it work better.

Dealing with Insects

Mosquito Repellent Pot

Place sawdust in metal pot or can and soak with kerosene. Light it on fire a while before your yard activities begin so the smoky kerosene smell has time to dissipate. This helps keep mosquitoes away so you can have a relaxing evening in your yard.

BETTY BYLER, Brockway, PA

Citronella for Bugs

To keep pesky flies and bugs away while camping, diffuse citronella oil in diffuser or burn a citronella candle.

MRS. GIDEON L. MILLER, Loudonville, OH

Citronella Floating Candle Bowl

1 tablespoon witch hazel
20 drops citronella
    essential oil
10 drops lemongrass
    essential oil
Water
Decorations of choice in
    2-inch sizes (optional)
1 unscented floating
    candle

Add witch hazel, citronella oil, and lemongrass oil to glass bowl. Fill with water. Place bowl outside on porch or picnic table. Add decorations to water, if desired, along with floating candle. Light candle to create cozy, pest-free environment.

AMANDA BYLER, Curwensville, PA

Quick Bug Deterrent

Open bottle of strong essential oil and place it in middle of picnic table to keep bugs away.

FANNIE S. BYLER, **New Wilmington, PA**

Easy Fly Trap

Fill plastic jar three-quarters full with water. Add ¼ cup apple cider vinegar, 2 tablespoons sugar, and 2 tablespoons dish soap. Use a very strong string and put ends down in jar, leaving string long enough for hanging. Screw on lid over string. Punch a few holes in lid so flies can get in. Hang jar on porch or other places around yard. Works amazingly well.

ESTHER MILLER, **Rossiter, PA**

Fly Spray

Put equal parts apple cider vinegar, Shaklee Basic-H, and water in spray bottle. Add 10 drops lavender oil. Use on any animals or surfaces to repel flies.

LOVINA GINGERICH, **Dalton, OH**

Total Ant Rid

Mix equal parts sugar and 20 Mule Team Borax. Spread around and against house. Kills all ants—from large black ants to tiny red ants.

ANNA A. SLABAUGH, **Apple Creek, OH**

Mosquito Repellent

10 to 15 drops citronella oil
Coconut oil

Put citronella oil in roller bottle and fill rest of bottle with coconut oil. Can also put in small spray bottle. To adjust scent, add peppermint oil.

Martha Mast, **North Bloomfield, OH**

Mosquito Spray

1 big bottle blue mouthwash
3 cups Epsom salt
3 (12 ounce) cans beer

Mix all ingredients well until salt is dissolved. Put in spray bottle and spray anywhere on lawn, flower beds, and flowers where mosquitoes may cluster in your area of play and relaxation.

Susanna Glick, **Bird-in-Hand, PA**

Natural Tick Repellent

2 cups water
10 drops clove essential oil
10 drops lavender essential oil

Put all ingredients in spray bottle and shake well. Spray on clothing, shoes, and wherever desired to keep ticks at bay. Shake bottle before each use.

Elsie Schlabach, **Big Prairie, OH**

Bug-Deterrent Plants

For a beautiful and bug-free back porch, patio, or campsite, plant lots of herbs. These grow well in pots or in the ground. Annuals that work well are marigolds, chrysanthemums, and petunias. Perennials that deter bugs include citronella grass, peppermint, spearmint, lavender, lemongrass, rosemary, chive, and basil. Also, neem oil works great to keep pesky mosquitoes and bugs away.

Kevin Miller Family, Shipshewana, IN

Essential Oil Bug Spray

Water	10 drops peppermint oil
Witch hazel	10 drops tea tree oil
10 drops lavender oil	20 drops lemongrass oil

Fill 4-ounce spray bottle half full with water. Add witch hazel to fill almost to top. Add lavender, peppermint, tea tree, and lemongrass oils. Close bottle and shake well before each use. Keeps mosquitoes away!

Esther Mast, Mercer, PA

I use either boiled water or distilled water, witch hazel, and 30 to 50 drops total of essential oils (citronella, clove, lemongrass, rosemary, tea tree, eucalyptus, cedar, lavender, and mint).
Fannie S. Byler, New Wilmington, PA

I use 30 to 50 drops essential oil. Approximately 10 drops clove, 10 drops rosemary, 30 drops total of lemongrass, tea tree, citronella, cedar, and/or lavender.
Barbara Detweiler, Quaker City, OH

The oils I use are 20 drops purification, 10 drops cedarwood (for ticks), 10 drops lavender, 5 drops geranium, 2 drops lemongrass, 2 drops basil, and 2 drops oregano added to 3 ounces water and 3 ounces witch hazel.
Mary King, New Holland, PA

Kids' Itch Stick

5 drops peppermint oil
5 drops purification oil
5 drops lavender oil

Carrier oil such as fractionated coconut oil

Combine oils in 10-milliliter roller bottle and fill up with carrier oil.

Amanda Byler, Curwensville, PA

Mosquito Bite Remedies

- Moisten bar of soap and rub on bite. It will relieve itching and act as disinfectant to prevent infection.

Mattie Petersheim, Junction City, OH

- Rub inside of banana peel over mosquito and other insect bites to reduce swelling and irritation. Also works for small burns to help keep from getting infected.

Mary Miller, Belmopan, Belize

Beesting Relief

For relief of beestings, rub a plantain (pig's ear) leaf on the sting until it quits hurting. It will also keep it from swelling. These leaves can be found in most yards.

Mrs. Josep Miller, Navarre, OH
Mrs. Joseph Schwartz, Berne, IN

Burned Tongue

If you burn your tongue on hot food or drink, put sugar on your tongue. It helps a lot.

Lydia A. Glick, Port Washington, OH

Index of Contributors

Index of Recipes by Key Ingredients